The

SIBLEY

BIRDER'S LIFE LIST & FIELD DIARY

———

DAVID ALLEN SIBLEY

CLARKSON POTTER/PUBLISHERS
NEW YORK

All rights reserved.
Published in the United States by Clarkson Potter/
Publishers, an imprint of the Crown Publishing Group,
a division of Penguin Random House LLC, New York.
crownpublishing.com
clarksonpotter.com

CLARKSON POTTER is a trademark and POTTER with
colophon is a registered trademark of Penguin Random
House LLC

ISBN 978-0-451-49745-1

Printed in China

Book and cover design by Danielle Deschenes
Cover illustrations by David Allen Sibley

10 9

First Edition

Contents

Introduction

In my guide *The Sibley Guide to Birds, Second Edition,* I stated that a small notebook and pencil is the best way to record details of your observations. Even in a digital age there is still great value in the act of writing and sketching. This field diary and life list is expressly designed to provide a lasting record of your experiences birdwatching.

This book includes three list formats. The first offers a detailed entry for each species in taxonomic sequence, with spaces to record the date and location of your first sighting, and a larger space for notes about your experiences. I wanted to leave the page relatively unstructured to allow you, the user, to develop whatever structure works for you. Everyone's life list is a personal thing, and these pages allow some freedom to personalize. The second list is a checklist in the same order, with boxes after each species listing for you to check off your sightings. The third is simply a series of numbered lines, where you can track your progress by entering species chronologically as they are added to your life list.

The sequence of families here follows the order described in the *Sibley Guide to Birds, Second Edition.* The species list offers space for recording the 990 species accepted in the North American region by the American Birding Association. The North American region includes the United States and Canada and all adjacent islands, but excludes Hawaii, Bermuda, and Greenland. Offshore waters are included to a distance of 200 miles (320 km) or halfway to the nearest land that is not part of the North American region, whichever is closer.

All species that have been verified as occurring naturally within this area are included, even if there is only one record, whereas *The Sibley Guide to Birds, Second Edition* excludes species that are very rare visitors to this continent. Also included in the main list here are all introduced species with established populations. Many additional exotic species can be seen regularly or occasionally in the wild, but have not established self-sustaining naturalized populations on this continent and are not included in the main list. The most frequently encountered species are illustrated in *The Sibley Guide to Birds, Second Edition,* and a separate list of these "non-established exotics" has been added at the end of the Species Listing and Checklist sections.

Recognizable regional variations of species are not included in this list. Many distinctive subspecies variations are illustrated and described in *The Sibley Guide to Birds, Second Edition,* but their classification is simply too subjective to be added to this list format. However, identifying and recording these subspecies variations is a very worthwhile and enlightening challenge, and I encourage you to add your own notations under each species when you see a distinctive subspecies variation. There are also blank templates at the end of the Species Listing, Checklist, and Life List sections, so you can add your own entries for additional species, regional variations, hybrids, etc.

Finally, do remember: Whether you are observing or photographing birds, it is important to avoid disturbing them whenever possible. Obey any posted rules and property boundaries, watch from a distance, and do not intentionally disturb birds. Keeping these simple courtesies in mind will benefit the birds and allow you to enjoy their unaltered natural behavior.

Ducks, Geese, and Swans

BLACK-BELLIED WHISTLING-DUCK	Date:
	Location:
Notes:	

FULVOUS WHISTLING-DUCK	Date:
	Location:
Notes:	

TAIGA BEAN-GOOSE ▲	Date:
	Location:
Notes:	

TUNDRA BEAN-GOOSE ▲	Date:
	Location:
Notes:	

PINK-FOOTED GOOSE ▲	Date:
	Location:
Notes:	

▲ RARE ■ EXTINCT

GREATER WHITE-FRONTED GOOSE	Date:
	Location:

Notes:

LESSER WHITE-FRONTED GOOSE ▲	Date:
	Location:

Notes:

GRAYLAG GOOSE	Date:
	Location:

Notes:

EMPEROR GOOSE	Date:
	Location:

Notes:

SNOW GOOSE	Date:
	Location:

Notes:

▲ RARE   ■ EXTINCT

Ducks, Geese, and Swans

ROSS'S GOOSE	Date:
	Location:
Notes:	

BRANT	Date:
	Location:
Notes:	

BARNACLE GOOSE ▲	Date:
	Location:
Notes:	

CACKLING GOOSE	Date:
	Location:
Notes:	

CANADA GOOSE	Date:
	Location:
Notes:	

▲ RARE ■ EXTINCT

MUTE SWAN	Date:
	Location:

Notes:

TRUMPETER SWAN	Date:
	Location:

Notes:

TUNDRA SWAN	Date:
	Location:

Notes:

WHOOPER SWAN ▲	Date:
	Location:

Notes:

EGYPTIAN GOOSE	Date:
	Location:

Notes:

▲ RARE   ■ EXTINCT

Ducks, Geese, and Swans

MUSCOVY DUCK	Date:
	Location:

Notes:

WOOD DUCK	Date:
	Location:

Notes:

GADWALL	Date:
	Location:

Notes:

FALCATED DUCK ▲	Date:
	Location:

Notes:

EURASIAN WIGEON	Date:
	Location:

Notes:

▲ RARE ■ EXTINCT

AMERICAN WIGEON	Date:
	Location:

Notes:

AMERICAN BLACK DUCK	Date:
	Location:

Notes:

MALLARD	Date:
	Location:

Notes:

MOTTLED DUCK	Date:
	Location:

Notes:

EASTERN SPOT-BILLED DUCK ▲	Date:
	Location:

Notes:

▲ RARE ■ EXTINCT

Ducks, Geese, and Swans

BLUE-WINGED TEAL	Date:
	Location:
Notes:	

CINNAMON TEAL	Date:
	Location:
Notes:	

NORTHERN SHOVELER	Date:
	Location:
Notes:	

WHITE-CHEEKED PINTAIL ▲	Date:
	Location:
Notes:	

NORTHERN PINTAIL	Date:
	Location:
Notes:	

▲ RARE   ■ EXTINCT

GARGANEY ▲	Date:
	Location:
Notes:	

BAIKAL TEAL ▲	Date:
	Location:
Notes:	

GREEN-WINGED TEAL	Date:
	Location:
Notes:	

CANVASBACK	Date:
	Location:
Notes:	

REDHEAD	Date:
	Location:
Notes:	

Ducks, Geese, and Swans

COMMON POCHARD ▲	Date:
	Location:
Notes:	

RING-NECKED DUCK	Date:
	Location:
Notes:	

TUFTED DUCK ▲	Date:
	Location:
Notes:	

GREATER SCAUP	Date:
	Location:
Notes:	

LESSER SCAUP	Date:
	Location:
Notes:	

▲ RARE   ■ EXTINCT

STELLER'S EIDER	Date:
	Location:

Notes:

SPECTACLED EIDER	Date:
	Location:

Notes:

KING EIDER	Date:
	Location:

Notes:

COMMON EIDER	Date:
	Location:

Notes:

HARLEQUIN DUCK	Date:
	Location:

Notes:

Ducks, Geese, and Swans

LABRADOR DUCK ■	Date:
	Location:
Notes:	

SURF SCOTER	Date:
	Location:
Notes:	

WHITE-WINGED SCOTER	Date:
	Location:
Notes:	

COMMON SCOTER ▲	Date:
	Location:
Notes:	

BLACK SCOTER	Date:
	Location:
Notes:	

▲ RARE ■ EXTINCT

LONG-TAILED DUCK	Date:
	Location:
Notes:	

BUFFLEHEAD	Date:
	Location:
Notes:	

COMMON GOLDENEYE	Date:
	Location:
Notes:	

BARROW'S GOLDENEYE	Date:
	Location:
Notes:	

SMEW ▲	Date:
	Location:
Notes:	

▲ RARE ■ EXTINCT

Ducks, Geese, and Swans

HOODED MERGANSER	Date:
	Location:
Notes:	

COMMON MERGANSER	Date:
	Location:
Notes:	

RED-BREASTED MERGANSER	Date:
	Location:
Notes:	

MASKED DUCK ▲	Date:
	Location:
Notes:	

RUDDY DUCK	Date:
	Location:
Notes:	

▲ RARE ■ EXTINCT

PLAIN CHACHALACA	Date:
	Location:
Notes:	

MOUNTAIN QUAIL	Date:
	Location:
Notes:	

SCALED QUAIL	Date:
	Location:
Notes:	

CALIFORNIA QUAIL	Date:
	Location:
Notes:	

GAMBEL'S QUAIL	Date:
	Location:
Notes:	

▲ RARE ■ EXTINCT

Quail

NORTHERN BOBWHITE	Date:
	Location:
Notes:	

MONTEZUMA QUAIL	Date:
	Location:
Notes:	

CHUKAR	Date:
	Location:
Notes:	

HIMALAYAN SNOWCOCK	Date:
	Location:
Notes:	

RING-NECKED PHEASANT	Date:
	Location:
Notes:	

▲ RARE ■ EXTINCT

GRAY PARTRIDGE	Date:
	Location:
Notes:	

RUFFED GROUSE	Date:
	Location:
Notes:	

GREATER SAGE-GROUSE	Date:
	Location:
Notes:	

GUNNISON SAGE-GROUSE	Date:
	Location:
Notes:	

SPRUCE GROUSE	Date:
	Location:
Notes:	

▲ RARE ■ EXTINCT

Pheasants

WILLOW PTARMIGAN	Date:
	Location:
Notes:	

ROCK PTARMIGAN	Date:
	Location:
Notes:	

WHITE-TAILED PTARMIGAN	Date:
	Location:
Notes:	

DUSKY GROUSE	Date:
	Location:
Notes:	

SOOTY GROUSE	Date:
	Location:
Notes:	

▲ RARE ■ EXTINCT

SHARP-TAILED GROUSE	Date:
	Location:

Notes:

GREATER PRAIRIE-CHICKEN	Date:
	Location:

Notes:

LESSER PRAIRIE-CHICKEN	Date:
	Location:

Notes:

WILD TURKEY	Date:
	Location:

Notes:

RED-THROATED LOON	Date:
	Location:

Notes:

▲ RARE ■ EXTINCT

Loons

ARCTIC LOON	Date:
	Location:
Notes:	

PACIFIC LOON	Date:
	Location:
Notes:	

COMMON LOON	Date:
	Location:
Notes:	

YELLOW-BILLED LOON	Date:
	Location:
Notes:	

LEAST GREBE	Date:
	Location:
Notes:	

▲ RARE ■ EXTINCT

PIED-BILLED GREBE	Date:
	Location:

Notes:

HORNED GREBE	Date:
	Location:

Notes:

RED-NECKED GREBE	Date:
	Location:

Notes:

EARED GREBE	Date:
	Location:

Notes:

WESTERN GREBE	Date:
	Location:

Notes:

Grebes

CLARK'S GREBE	Date:
	Location:
Notes:	

AMERICAN FLAMINGO ▲	Date:
	Location:
Notes:	

YELLOW-NOSED ALBATROSS ▲	Date:
	Location:
Notes:	

WHITE-CAPPED ALBATROSS ▲	Date:
	Location:
Notes:	

SALVIN'S ALBATROSS ▲	Date:
	Location:
Notes:	

▲ RARE ■ EXTINCT

BLACK-BROWED ALBATROSS ▲	Date:
	Location:
Notes:	

LIGHT-MANTLED ALBATROSS ▲	Date:
	Location:
Notes:	

WANDERING ALBATROSS ▲	Date:
	Location:
Notes:	

LAYSAN ALBATROSS	Date:
	Location:
Notes:	

BLACK-FOOTED ALBATROSS	Date:
	Location:
Notes:	

Albatrosses

SHORT-TAILED ALBATROSS ▲	Date:
	Location:
Notes:	

NORTHERN FULMAR	Date:
	Location:
Notes:	

GREAT-WINGED PETREL ▲	Date:
	Location:
Notes:	

TRINDADE PETREL ▲	Date:
	Location:
Notes:	

MURPHY'S PETREL ▲	Date:
	Location:
Notes:	

▲ RARE ■ EXTINCT

PROVIDENCE PETREL ▲	Date:
	Location:
Notes:	

ZINO'S PETREL ▲	Date:
	Location:
Notes:	

FEA'S PETREL ▲	Date:
	Location:
Notes:	

MOTTLED PETREL ▲	Date:
	Location:
Notes:	

BERMUDA PETREL ▲	Date:
	Location:
Notes:	

Shearwaters and Petrels

BLACK-CAPPED PETREL	Date:
	Location:
Notes:	

HAWAIIAN PETREL ▲	Date:
	Location:
Notes:	

COOK'S PETREL ▲	Date:
	Location:
Notes:	

STEJNEGER'S PETREL ▲	Date:
	Location:
Notes:	

BULWER'S PETREL ▲	Date:
	Location:
Notes:	

WHITE-CHINNED PETREL ▲	Date:
	Location:
Notes:	

PARKINSON'S PETREL ▲	Date:
	Location:
Notes:	

STREAKED SHEARWATER ▲	Date:
	Location:
Notes:	

CORY'S SHEARWATER	Date:
	Location:
Notes:	

CAPE VERDE SHEARWATER ▲	Date:
	Location:
Notes:	

▲ RARE ■ EXTINCT

Shearwaters and Petrels

PINK-FOOTED SHEARWATER	Date:
	Location:
Notes:	

FLESH-FOOTED SHEARWATER	Date:
	Location:
Notes:	

GREAT SHEARWATER	Date:
	Location:
Notes:	

WEDGE-TAILED SHEARWATER ▲	Date:
	Location:
Notes:	

BULLER'S SHEARWATER	Date:
	Location:
Notes:	

▲ RARE ■ EXTINCT

SOOTY SHEARWATER	Date:
	Location:
Notes:	

SHORT-TAILED SHEARWATER	Date:
	Location:
Notes:	

MANX SHEARWATER	Date:
	Location:
Notes:	

NEWELL'S SHEARWATER ▲	Date:
	Location:
Notes:	

BLACK-VENTED SHEARWATER	Date:
	Location:
Notes:	

Shearwaters and Petrels

BAROLO SHEARWATER ▲	Date:
	Location:
Notes:	

AUDUBON'S SHEARWATER	Date:
	Location:
Notes:	

WILSON'S STORM-PETREL	Date:
	Location:
Notes:	

WHITE-FACED STORM-PETREL ▲	Date:
	Location:
Notes:	

EUROPEAN STORM-PETREL ▲	Date:
	Location:
Notes:	

▲ RARE   ■ EXTINCT

BLACK-BELLIED STORM-PETREL ▲	Date:
	Location:

Notes:

FORK-TAILED STORM-PETREL	Date:
	Location:

Notes:

RINGED STORM-PETREL ▲	Date:
	Location:

Notes:

LEACH'S STORM-PETREL	Date:
	Location:

Notes:

SWINHOE'S STORM-PETREL ▲	Date:
	Location:

Notes:

▲ RARE ■ EXTINCT

Shearwaters and Petrels

ASHY STORM-PETREL	Date:
	Location:
Notes:	

BAND-RUMPED STORM-PETREL	Date:
	Location:
Notes:	

WEDGE-RUMPED STORM-PETREL ▲	Date:
	Location:
Notes:	

BLACK STORM-PETREL	Date:
	Location:
Notes:	

TRISTRAM'S STORM-PETREL ▲	Date:
	Location:
Notes:	

▲ RARE   ■ EXTINCT

LEAST STORM-PETREL	Date:
	Location:
Notes:	

WHITE-TAILED TROPICBIRD ▲	Date:
	Location:
Notes:	

RED-BILLED TROPICBIRD ▲	Date:
	Location:
Notes:	

RED-TAILED TROPICBIRD ▲	Date:
	Location:
Notes:	

JABIRU ▲	Date:
	Location:
Notes:	

▲ RARE ■ EXTINCT

Wood Stork and Jabiru

WOOD STORK	Date:
	Location:
Notes:	

LESSER FRIGATEBIRD ▲	Date:
	Location:
Notes:	

MAGNIFICENT FRIGATEBIRD	Date:
	Location:
Notes:	

GREAT FRIGATEBIRD ▲	Date:
	Location:
Notes:	

MASKED BOOBY	Date:
	Location:
Notes:	

▲ RARE ■ EXTINCT

BLUE-FOOTED BOOBY ▲	Date:
	Location:
Notes:	

BROWN BOOBY	Date:
	Location:
Notes:	

RED-FOOTED BOOBY ▲	Date:
	Location:
Notes:	

NORTHERN GANNET	Date:
	Location:
Notes:	

BRANDT'S CORMORANT	Date:
	Location:
Notes:	

Cormorants

NEOTROPIC CORMORANT	Date:
	Location:
Notes:	

DOUBLE-CRESTED CORMORANT	Date:
	Location:
Notes:	

GREAT CORMORANT	Date:
	Location:
Notes:	

RED-FACED CORMORANT	Date:
	Location:
Notes:	

PELAGIC CORMORANT	Date:
	Location:
Notes:	

▲ RARE ■ EXTINCT

ANHINGA	Date:
	Location:
Notes:	

AMERICAN WHITE PELICAN	Date:
	Location:
Notes:	

BROWN PELICAN	Date:
	Location:
Notes:	

AMERICAN BITTERN	Date:
	Location:
Notes:	

YELLOW BITTERN ▲	Date:
	Location:
Notes:	

Bitterns, Herons, and Egrets

LEAST BITTERN	Date:
	Location:
Notes:	

BARE-THROATED TIGER-HERON ▲	Date:
	Location:
Notes:	

GREAT BLUE HERON	Date:
	Location:
Notes:	

GRAY HERON ▲	Date:
	Location:
Notes:	

GREAT EGRET	Date:
	Location:
Notes:	

▲ RARE ■ EXTINCT

INTERMEDIATE EGRET ▲	Date:
	Location:

Notes:

CHINESE EGRET ▲	Date:
	Location:

Notes:

LITTLE EGRET ▲	Date:
	Location:

Notes:

WESTERN REEF-HERON ▲	Date:
	Location:

Notes:

SNOWY EGRET	Date:
	Location:

Notes:

Bitterns, Herons, and Egrets

LITTLE BLUE HERON	Date:
	Location:
Notes:	

TRICOLORED HERON	Date:
	Location:
Notes:	

REDDISH EGRET	Date:
	Location:
Notes:	

CATTLE EGRET	Date:
	Location:
Notes:	

CHINESE POND-HERON ▲	Date:
	Location:
Notes:	

▲ RARE ■ EXTINCT

GREEN HERON	Date:
	Location:

Notes:

BLACK-CROWNED NIGHT-HERON	Date:
	Location:

Notes:

YELLOW-CROWNED NIGHT-HERON	Date:
	Location:

Notes:

WHITE IBIS	Date:
	Location:

Notes:

SCARLET IBIS ▲	Date:
	Location:

Notes:

▲ RARE ■ EXTINCT

Ibises and Roseate Spoonbill

GLOSSY IBIS	Date:
	Location:
Notes:	

WHITE-FACED IBIS	Date:
	Location:
Notes:	

ROSEATE SPOONBILL	Date:
	Location:
Notes:	

BLACK VULTURE	Date:
	Location:
Notes:	

TURKEY VULTURE	Date:
	Location:
Notes:	

▲ RARE ■ EXTINCT

CALIFORNIA CONDOR	Date:
	Location:
Notes:	

OSPREY	Date:
	Location:
Notes:	

WHITE-TAILED KITE	Date:
	Location:
Notes:	

HOOK-BILLED KITE	Date:
	Location:
Notes:	

SWALLOW-TAILED KITE	Date:
	Location:
Notes:	

▲ RARE ■ EXTINCT

Hawks and Eagles

GOLDEN EAGLE	Date:
	Location:
Notes:	

SNAIL KITE	Date:
	Location:
Notes:	

DOUBLE-TOOTHED KITE ▲	Date:
	Location:
Notes:	

MISSISSIPPI KITE	Date:
	Location:
Notes:	

NORTHERN HARRIER	Date:
	Location:
Notes:	

▲ RARE ■ EXTINCT

SHARP-SHINNED HAWK	Date:
	Location:
Notes:	

COOPER'S HAWK	Date:
	Location:
Notes:	

NORTHERN GOSHAWK	Date:
	Location:
Notes:	

BALD EAGLE	Date:
	Location:
Notes:	

WHITE-TAILED EAGLE ▲	Date:
	Location:
Notes:	

Hawks and Eagles

STELLER'S SEA-EAGLE ▲	Date:
	Location:
Notes:	

CRANE HAWK ▲	Date:
	Location:
Notes:	

COMMON BLACK HAWK	Date:
	Location:
Notes:	

ROADSIDE HAWK ▲	Date:
	Location:
Notes:	

HARRIS'S HAWK	Date:
	Location:
Notes:	

▲ RARE ■ EXTINCT

WHITE-TAILED HAWK	Date:
	Location:
Notes:	

GRAY HAWK	Date:
	Location:
Notes:	

RED-SHOULDERED HAWK	Date:
	Location:
Notes:	

BROAD-WINGED HAWK	Date:
	Location:
Notes:	

SHORT-TAILED HAWK	Date:
	Location:
Notes:	

Hawks and Eagles

SWAINSON'S HAWK	Date:
	Location:
Notes:	

ZONE-TAILED HAWK	Date:
	Location:
Notes:	

RED-TAILED HAWK	Date:
	Location:
Notes:	

ROUGH-LEGGED HAWK	Date:
	Location:
Notes:	

FERRUGINOUS HAWK	Date:
	Location:
Notes:	

▲ RARE ■ EXTINCT

YELLOW RAIL	Date:
	Location:

Notes:

BLACK RAIL	Date:
	Location:

Notes:

CORN CRAKE ▲	Date:
	Location:

Notes:

RIDGWAY'S RAIL	Date:
	Location:

Notes:

KING RAIL	Date:
	Location:

Notes:

▲ RARE ■ EXTINCT

Rails and Coots

CLAPPER RAIL	Date:
	Location:
Notes:	

VIRGINIA RAIL	Date:
	Location:
Notes:	

RUFOUS-NECKED WOOD-RAIL ▲	Date:
	Location:
Notes:	

SORA	Date:
	Location:
Notes:	

PAINT-BILLED CRAKE ▲	Date:
	Location:
Notes:	

▲ RARE   ■ EXTINCT

SPOTTED RAIL ▲	Date:
	Location:

Notes:

PURPLE GALLINULE	Date:
	Location:

Notes:

PURPLE SWAMPHEN	Date:
	Location:

Notes:

COMMON MOORHEN ▲	Date:
	Location:

Notes:

COMMON GALLINULE	Date:
	Location:

Notes:

Rails and Coots

EURASIAN COOT ▲	Date:
	Location:
Notes:	

AMERICAN COOT	Date:
	Location:
Notes:	

SUNGREBE ▲	Date:
	Location:
Notes:	

LIMPKIN	Date:
	Location:
Notes:	

SANDHILL CRANE	Date:
	Location:
Notes:	

COMMON CRANE ▲	Date:
	Location:
Notes:	

WHOOPING CRANE	Date:
	Location:
Notes:	

DOUBLE-STRIPED THICK-KNEE ▲	Date:
	Location:
Notes:	

BLACK-WINGED STILT ▲	Date:
	Location:
Notes:	

BLACK-NECKED STILT	Date:
	Location:
Notes:	

▲ RARE ■ EXTINCT

Avocets and Stilts

AMERICAN AVOCET	Date:
	Location:
Notes:	

EURASIAN OYSTERCATCHER ▲	Date:
	Location:
Notes:	

AMERICAN OYSTERCATCHER	Date:
	Location:
Notes:	

BLACK OYSTERCATCHER	Date:
	Location:
Notes:	

BLACK-BELLIED PLOVER	Date:
	Location:
Notes:	

▲ RARE ■ EXTINCT

EUROPEAN GOLDEN-PLOVER ▲	Date:
	Location:
Notes:	

AMERICAN GOLDEN-PLOVER	Date:
	Location:
Notes:	

PACIFIC GOLDEN-PLOVER	Date:
	Location:
Notes:	

NORTHERN LAPWING ▲	Date:
	Location:
Notes:	

LESSER SAND-PLOVER ▲	Date:
	Location:
Notes:	

▲ RARE ■ EXTINCT

Plovers

GREATER SAND-PLOVER ▲	Date:
	Location:
Notes:	

COLLARED PLOVER ▲	Date:
	Location:
Notes:	

SNOWY PLOVER	Date:
	Location:
Notes:	

WILSON'S PLOVER	Date:
	Location:
Notes:	

COMMON RINGED PLOVER	Date:
	Location:
Notes:	

▲ RARE ■ EXTINCT

SEMIPALMATED PLOVER	Date:
	Location:
Notes:	

PIPING PLOVER	Date:
	Location:
Notes:	

LITTLE RINGED PLOVER ▲	Date:
	Location:
Notes:	

KILLDEER	Date:
	Location:
Notes:	

MOUNTAIN PLOVER	Date:
	Location:
Notes:	

Plovers

EURASIAN DOTTEREL ▲	Date:
	Location:
Notes:	

NORTHERN JACANA ▲	Date:
	Location:
Notes:	

TEREK SANDPIPER ▲	Date:
	Location:
Notes:	

COMMON SANDPIPER ▲	Date:
	Location:
Notes:	

SPOTTED SANDPIPER	Date:
	Location:
Notes:	

▲ RARE ■ EXTINCT

GREEN SANDPIPER ▲	Date:
	Location:
Notes:	

SOLITARY SANDPIPER	Date:
	Location:
Notes:	

GRAY-TAILED TATTLER ▲	Date:
	Location:
Notes:	

WANDERING TATTLER	Date:
	Location:
Notes:	

SPOTTED REDSHANK ▲	Date:
	Location:
Notes:	

▲ RARE ■ EXTINCT

Sandpipers

GREATER YELLOWLEGS	Date:
	Location:
Notes:	

COMMON GREENSHANK ▲	Date:
	Location:
Notes:	

WILLET	Date:
	Location:
Notes:	

LESSER YELLOWLEGS	Date:
	Location:
Notes:	

MARSH SANDPIPER ▲	Date:
	Location:
Notes:	

▲ RARE ■ EXTINCT

WOOD SANDPIPER ▲	Date:
	Location:
Notes:	

COMMON REDSHANK ▲	Date:
	Location:
Notes:	

UPLAND SANDPIPER	Date:
	Location:
Notes:	

LITTLE CURLEW ▲	Date:
	Location:
Notes:	

ESKIMO CURLEW ■	Date:
	Location:
Notes:	

▲ RARE ■ EXTINCT

Sandpipers

WHIMBREL	Date:
	Location:

Notes:

BRISTLE-THIGHED CURLEW	Date:
	Location:

Notes:

FAR EASTERN CURLEW ▲	Date:
	Location:

Notes:

SLENDER-BILLED CURLEW ▲	Date:
	Location:

Notes:

EURASIAN CURLEW ▲	Date:
	Location:

Notes:

▲ RARE ■ EXTINCT

LONG-BILLED CURLEW	Date:
	Location:
Notes:	

BLACK-TAILED GODWIT ▲	Date:
	Location:
Notes:	

HUDSONIAN GODWIT	Date:
	Location:
Notes:	

BAR-TAILED GODWIT	Date:
	Location:
Notes:	

MARBLED GODWIT	Date:
	Location:
Notes:	

▲ RARE ■ EXTINCT

Sandpipers

RUDDY TURNSTONE	Date:
	Location:
Notes:	

BLACK TURNSTONE	Date:
	Location:
Notes:	

GREAT KNOT ▲	Date:
	Location:
Notes:	

RED KNOT	Date:
	Location:
Notes:	

SURFBIRD	Date:
	Location:
Notes:	

▲ RARE ■ EXTINCT

RUFF ▲	Date:
	Location:

Notes:

BROAD-BILLED SANDPIPER ▲	Date:
	Location:

Notes:

SHARP-TAILED SANDPIPER ▲	Date:
	Location:

Notes:

STILT SANDPIPER	Date:
	Location:

Notes:

CURLEW SANDPIPER ▲	Date:
	Location:

Notes:

▲ RARE   ■ EXTINCT

Sandpipers

TEMMINCK'S STINT ▲	Date:
	Location:
Notes:	

LONG-TOED STINT ▲	Date:
	Location:
Notes:	

SPOON-BILLED SANDPIPER ▲	Date:
	Location:
Notes:	

RED-NECKED STINT ▲	Date:
	Location:
Notes:	

SANDERLING	Date:
	Location:
Notes:	

▲ RARE ■ EXTINCT

DUNLIN	Date:
	Location:

Notes:

ROCK SANDPIPER	Date:
	Location:

Notes:

PURPLE SANDPIPER	Date:
	Location:

Notes:

BAIRD'S SANDPIPER	Date:
	Location:

Notes:

LITTLE STINT ▲	Date:
	Location:

Notes:

▲ RARE ■ EXTINCT

Sandpipers

LEAST SANDPIPER	Date:
	Location:
Notes:	

WHITE-RUMPED SANDPIPER	Date:
	Location:
Notes:	

BUFF-BREASTED SANDPIPER	Date:
	Location:
Notes:	

PECTORAL SANDPIPER	Date:
	Location:
Notes:	

SEMIPALMATED SANDPIPER	Date:
	Location:
Notes:	

▲ RARE ■ EXTINCT

WESTERN SANDPIPER	Date:
	Location:
Notes:	

SHORT-BILLED DOWITCHER	Date:
	Location:
Notes:	

LONG-BILLED DOWITCHER	Date:
	Location:
Notes:	

JACK SNIPE ▲	Date:
	Location:
Notes:	

SOLITARY SNIPE ▲	Date:
	Location:
Notes:	

Sandpipers

WILSON'S SNIPE	Date:
	Location:
Notes:	

COMMON SNIPE ▲	Date:
	Location:
Notes:	

PIN-TAILED SNIPE ▲	Date:
	Location:
Notes:	

EURASIAN WOODCOCK ▲	Date:
	Location:
Notes:	

AMERICAN WOODCOCK	Date:
	Location:
Notes:	

▲ RARE   ■ EXTINCT

WILSON'S PHALAROPE	Date:
	Location:
Notes:	

RED-NECKED PHALAROPE	Date:
	Location:
Notes:	

RED PHALAROPE	Date:
	Location:
Notes:	

ORIENTAL PRATINCOLE ▲	Date:
	Location:
Notes:	

GREAT SKUA	Date:
	Location:
Notes:	

▲ RARE   ■ EXTINCT

Skuas and Jaegers

SOUTH POLAR SKUA	Date:
	Location:
Notes:	

POMARINE JAEGER	Date:
	Location:
Notes:	

PARASITIC JAEGER	Date:
	Location:
Notes:	

LONG-TAILED JAEGER	Date:
	Location:
Notes:	

DOVEKIE	Date:
	Location:
Notes:	

▲ RARE ■ EXTINCT

COMMON MURRE	Date:
	Location:
Notes:	

THICK-BILLED MURRE	Date:
	Location:
Notes:	

RAZORBILL	Date:
	Location:
Notes:	

GREAT AUK ■	Date:
	Location:
Notes:	

BLACK GUILLEMOT	Date:
	Location:
Notes:	

Alcids

PIGEON GUILLEMOT	Date:
	Location:
Notes:	

LONG-BILLED MURRELET ▲	Date:
	Location:
Notes:	

MARBLED MURRELET	Date:
	Location:
Notes:	

KITTLITZ'S MURRELET	Date:
	Location:
Notes:	

SCRIPPS'S MURRELET	Date:
	Location:
Notes:	

▲ RARE ■ EXTINCT

GUADALUPE MURRELET ▲	Date:
	Location:

Notes:

CRAVERI'S MURRELET ▲	Date:
	Location:

Notes:

ANCIENT MURRELET	Date:
	Location:

Notes:

CASSIN'S AUKLET	Date:
	Location:

Notes:

PARAKEET AUKLET	Date:
	Location:

Notes:

Alcids

LEAST AUKLET	Date:
	Location:
Notes:	

WHISKERED AUKLET	Date:
	Location:
Notes:	

CRESTED AUKLET	Date:
	Location:
Notes:	

RHINOCEROS AUKLET	Date:
	Location:
Notes:	

ATLANTIC PUFFIN	Date:
	Location:
Notes:	

▲ RARE ■ EXTINCT

HORNED PUFFIN	Date:
	Location:
Notes:	

TUFTED PUFFIN	Date:
	Location:
Notes:	

SWALLOW-TAILED GULL ▲	Date:
	Location:
Notes:	

BLACK-LEGGED KITTIWAKE	Date:
	Location:
Notes:	

RED-LEGGED KITTIWAKE	Date:
	Location:
Notes:	

▲ RARE ■ EXTINCT

IVORY GULL	Date:
	Location:
Notes:	

SABINE'S GULL	Date:
	Location:
Notes:	

BONAPARTE'S GULL	Date:
	Location:
Notes:	

GRAY-HOODED GULL ▲	Date:
	Location:
Notes:	

BLACK-HEADED GULL	Date:
	Location:
Notes:	

▲ RARE ■ EXTINCT

LITTLE GULL	Date:
	Location:

Notes:

ROSS'S GULL	Date:
	Location:

Notes:

LAUGHING GULL	Date:
	Location:

Notes:

FRANKLIN'S GULL	Date:
	Location:

Notes:

BELCHER'S GULL ▲	Date:
	Location:

Notes:

▲ RARE   ■ EXTINCT

Gulls, Terns, and Skimmer

BLACK-TAILED GULL ▲	Date:
	Location:
Notes:	

HEERMANN'S GULL	Date:
	Location:
Notes:	

MEW GULL	Date:
	Location:
Notes:	

RING-BILLED GULL	Date:
	Location:
Notes:	

WESTERN GULL	Date:
	Location:
Notes:	

YELLOW-FOOTED GULL	Date:
	Location:
Notes:	

CALIFORNIA GULL	Date:
	Location:
Notes:	

HERRING GULL	Date:
	Location:
Notes:	

YELLOW-LEGGED GULL ▲	Date:
	Location:
Notes:	

THAYER'S GULL	Date:
	Location:
Notes:	

Gulls, Terns, and Skimmer

ICELAND GULL	Date:
	Location:
Notes:	

LESSER BLACK-BACKED GULL	Date:
	Location:
Notes:	

SLATY-BACKED GULL	Date:
	Location:
Notes:	

GLAUCOUS-WINGED GULL	Date:
	Location:
Notes:	

GLAUCOUS GULL	Date:
	Location:
Notes:	

▲ RARE ■ EXTINCT

GREAT BLACK-BACKED GULL

Date:

Location:

Notes:

KELP GULL ▲

Date:

Location:

Notes:

BROWN NODDY

Date:

Location:

Notes:

BLACK NODDY ▲

Date:

Location:

Notes:

SOOTY TERN

Date:

Location:

Notes:

BRIDLED TERN	Date:
	Location:
Notes:	

ALEUTIAN TERN	Date:
	Location:
Notes:	

LEAST TERN	Date:
	Location:
Notes:	

LARGE-BILLED TERN ▲	Date:
	Location:
Notes:	

GULL-BILLED TERN	Date:
	Location:
Notes:	

▲ RARE ■ EXTINCT

CASPIAN TERN	Date:
	Location:
Notes:	

BLACK TERN	Date:
	Location:
Notes:	

WHITE-WINGED TERN ▲	Date:
	Location:
Notes:	

WHISKERED TERN ▲	Date:
	Location:
Notes:	

ROSEATE TERN	Date:
	Location:
Notes:	

Gulls, Terns, and Skimmer

COMMON TERN	Date:
	Location:
Notes:	

ARCTIC TERN	Date:
	Location:
Notes:	

FORSTER'S TERN	Date:
	Location:
Notes:	

ROYAL TERN	Date:
	Location:
Notes:	

SANDWICH TERN	Date:
	Location:
Notes:	

ELEGANT TERN	Date:
	Location:
Notes:	

BLACK SKIMMER	Date:
	Location:
Notes:	

ROCK PIGEON	Date:
	Location:
Notes:	

SCALY-NAPED PIGEON ▲	Date:
	Location:
Notes:	

WHITE-CROWNED PIGEON	Date:
	Location:
Notes:	

Pigeons and Doves

RED-BILLED PIGEON	Date:
	Location:
Notes:	

BAND-TAILED PIGEON	Date:
	Location:
Notes:	

PASSENGER PIGEON ■	Date:
	Location:
Notes:	

EUROPEAN TURTLE-DOVE ▲	Date:
	Location:
Notes:	

ORIENTAL TURTLE-DOVE ▲	Date:
	Location:
Notes:	

EURASIAN COLLARED-DOVE	Date:
	Location:

Notes:

AFRICAN COLLARED-DOVE	Date:
	Location:

Notes:

SPOTTED DOVE	Date:
	Location:

Notes:

INCA DOVE	Date:
	Location:

Notes:

COMMON GROUND-DOVE	Date:
	Location:

Notes:

▲ RARE ■ EXTINCT

Pigeons and Doves

RUDDY GROUND-DOVE	Date:
	Location:
Notes:	

RUDDY QUAIL-DOVE ▲	Date:
	Location:
Notes:	

KEY WEST QUAIL-DOVE ▲	Date:
	Location:
Notes:	

WHITE-TIPPED DOVE	Date:
	Location:
Notes:	

WHITE-WINGED DOVE	Date:
	Location:
Notes:	

▲ RARE ■ EXTINCT

ZENAIDA DOVE ▲	Date:
	Location:

Notes:

MOURNING DOVE	Date:
	Location:

Notes:

COMMON CUCKOO ▲	Date:
	Location:

Notes:

ORIENTAL CUCKOO ▲	Date:
	Location:

Notes:

YELLOW-BILLED CUCKOO	Date:
	Location:

Notes:

▲ RARE ■ EXTINCT

Cuckoos

MANGROVE CUCKOO	Date:
	Location:
Notes:	

BLACK-BILLED CUCKOO	Date:
	Location:
Notes:	

GREATER ROADRUNNER	Date:
	Location:
Notes:	

SMOOTH-BILLED ANI ▲	Date:
	Location:
Notes:	

GROOVE-BILLED ANI	Date:
	Location:
Notes:	

▲ RARE ■ EXTINCT

BARN OWL	Date:
	Location:
Notes:	

ORIENTAL SCOPS-OWL ▲	Date:
	Location:
Notes:	

FLAMMULATED OWL	Date:
	Location:
Notes:	

WESTERN SCREECH-OWL	Date:
	Location:
Notes:	

EASTERN SCREECH-OWL	Date:
	Location:
Notes:	

▲ RARE ■ EXTINCT

WHISKERED SCREECH-OWL	Date:
	Location:

Notes:

GREAT HORNED OWL	Date:
	Location:

Notes:

SNOWY OWL	Date:
	Location:

Notes:

NORTHERN HAWK OWL	Date:
	Location:

Notes:

NORTHERN PYGMY-OWL	Date:
	Location:

Notes:

▲ RARE ■ EXTINCT

FERRUGINOUS PYGMY-OWL	Date:
	Location:

Notes:

ELF OWL	Date:
	Location:

Notes:

BURROWING OWL	Date:
	Location:

Notes:

MOTTLED OWL ▲	Date:
	Location:

Notes:

SPOTTED OWL	Date:
	Location:

Notes:

Owls

BARRED OWL	Date:
	Location:
Notes:	

GREAT GRAY OWL	Date:
	Location:
Notes:	

LONG-EARED OWL	Date:
	Location:
Notes:	

STYGIAN OWL ▲	Date:
	Location:
Notes:	

SHORT-EARED OWL	Date:
	Location:
Notes:	

▲ RARE ■ EXTINCT

BOREAL OWL	Date:
	Location:

Notes:

NORTHERN SAW-WHET OWL	Date:
	Location:

Notes:

NORTHERN BOOBOOK ▲	Date:
	Location:

Notes:

LESSER NIGHTHAWK	Date:
	Location:

Notes:

COMMON NIGHTHAWK	Date:
	Location:

Notes:

Nightjars

ANTILLEAN NIGHTHAWK	Date:
	Location:
Notes:	

COMMON PAURAQUE	Date:
	Location:
Notes:	

COMMON POORWILL	Date:
	Location:
Notes:	

CHUCK-WILL'S-WIDOW	Date:
	Location:
Notes:	

BUFF-COLLARED NIGHTJAR	Date:
	Location:
Notes:	

▲ RARE ■ EXTINCT

EASTERN WHIP-POOR-WILL	Date:
	Location:
Notes:	

MEXICAN WHIP-POOR-WILL	Date:
	Location:
Notes:	

GRAY NIGHTJAR ▲	Date:
	Location:
Notes:	

BLACK SWIFT	Date:
	Location:
Notes:	

WHITE-COLLARED SWIFT ▲	Date:
	Location:
Notes:	

▲ RARE ■ EXTINCT

Swifts

CHIMNEY SWIFT	Date:
	Location:
Notes:	

VAUX'S SWIFT	Date:
	Location:
Notes:	

WHITE-THROATED NEEDLETAIL ▲	Date:
	Location:
Notes:	

COMMON SWIFT ▲	Date:
	Location:
Notes:	

FORK-TAILED SWIFT ▲	Date:
	Location:
Notes:	

▲ RARE   ■ EXTINCT

WHITE-THROATED SWIFT	Date:
	Location:
Notes:	

ANTILLEAN PALM-SWIFT ▲	Date:
	Location:
Notes:	

GREEN VIOLETEAR ▲	Date:
	Location:
Notes:	

GREEN-BREASTED MANGO ▲	Date:
	Location:
Notes:	

MAGNIFICENT HUMMINGBIRD	Date:
	Location:
Notes:	

▲ RARE ■ EXTINCT

Hummingbirds

PLAIN-CAPPED STARTHROAT ▲	Date:
	Location:
Notes:	

BLUE-THROATED HUMMINGBIRD	Date:
	Location:
Notes:	

LUCIFER HUMMINGBIRD	Date:
	Location:
Notes:	

BAHAMA WOODSTAR ▲	Date:
	Location:
Notes:	

RUBY-THROATED HUMMINGBIRD	Date:
	Location:
Notes:	

▲ RARE ■ EXTINCT

BLACK-CHINNED HUMMINGBIRD	Date:
	Location:

Notes:

ANNA'S HUMMINGBIRD	Date:
	Location:

Notes:

COSTA'S HUMMINGBIRD	Date:
	Location:

Notes:

BUMBLEBEE HUMMINGBIRD ▲	Date:
	Location:

Notes:

BROAD-TAILED HUMMINGBIRD	Date:
	Location:

Notes:

▲ RARE ■ EXTINCT

Hummingbirds

RUFOUS HUMMINGBIRD	Date:
	Location:
Notes:	

ALLEN'S HUMMINGBIRD	Date:
	Location:
Notes:	

CALLIOPE HUMMINGBIRD	Date:
	Location:
Notes:	

BROAD-BILLED HUMMINGBIRD	Date:
	Location:
Notes:	

BERYLLINE HUMMINGBIRD ▲	Date:
	Location:
Notes:	

▲ RARE ■ EXTINCT

BUFF-BELLIED HUMMINGBIRD	Date:
	Location:

Notes:

CINNAMON HUMMINGBIRD ▲	Date:
	Location:

Notes:

VIOLET-CROWNED HUMMINGBIRD	Date:
	Location:

Notes:

WHITE-EARED HUMMINGBIRD	Date:
	Location:

Notes:

XANTUS'S HUMMINGBIRD ▲	Date:
	Location:

Notes:

▲ RARE ■ EXTINCT

Hummingbirds

EARED QUETZAL ▲	Date:
	Location:
Notes:	

ELEGANT TROGON	Date:
	Location:
Notes:	

EURASIAN HOOPOE ▲	Date:
	Location:
Notes:	

RINGED KINGFISHER	Date:
	Location:
Notes:	

BELTED KINGFISHER	Date:
	Location:
Notes:	

▲ RARE ■ EXTINCT

AMAZON KINGFISHER ▲	Date:
	Location:

Notes:

GREEN KINGFISHER	Date:
	Location:

Notes:

EURASIAN WRYNECK ▲	Date:
	Location:

Notes:

LEWIS'S WOODPECKER	Date:
	Location:

Notes:

RED-HEADED WOODPECKER	Date:
	Location:

Notes:

▲ RARE ■ EXTINCT

Woodpeckers

ACORN WOODPECKER	Date:
	Location:
Notes:	

GILA WOODPECKER	Date:
	Location:
Notes:	

GOLDEN-FRONTED WOODPECKER	Date:
	Location:
Notes:	

RED-BELLIED WOODPECKER	Date:
	Location:
Notes:	

WILLIAMSON'S SAPSUCKER	Date:
	Location:
Notes:	

▲ RARE ■ EXTINCT

YELLOW-BELLIED SAPSUCKER	Date:
	Location:
Notes:	

RED-NAPED SAPSUCKER	Date:
	Location:
Notes:	

RED-BREASTED SAPSUCKER	Date:
	Location:
Notes:	

GREAT SPOTTED WOODPECKER ▲	Date:
	Location:
Notes:	

LADDER-BACKED WOODPECKER	Date:
	Location:
Notes:	

▲ RARE ■ EXTINCT

Woodpeckers

NUTTALL'S WOODPECKER	Date:
	Location:
Notes:	

DOWNY WOODPECKER	Date:
	Location:
Notes:	

HAIRY WOODPECKER	Date:
	Location:
Notes:	

ARIZONA WOODPECKER	Date:
	Location:
Notes:	

RED-COCKADED WOODPECKER	Date:
	Location:
Notes:	

WHITE-HEADED WOODPECKER	Date:
	Location:

Notes:

AMERICAN THREE-TOED WOODPECKER	Date:
	Location:

Notes:

BLACK-BACKED WOODPECKER	Date:
	Location:

Notes:

NORTHERN FLICKER	Date:
	Location:

Notes:

GILDED FLICKER	Date:
	Location:

Notes:

Woodpeckers

PILEATED WOODPECKER	Date:
	Location:
Notes:	

IVORY-BILLED WOODPECKER ■	Date:
	Location:
Notes:	

COLLARED FOREST-FALCON ▲	Date:
	Location:
Notes:	

CRESTED CARACARA	Date:
	Location:
Notes:	

EURASIAN KESTREL ▲	Date:
	Location:
Notes:	

▲ RARE ■ EXTINCT

AMERICAN KESTREL	Date:
	Location:
Notes:	

RED-FOOTED FALCON ▲	Date:
	Location:
Notes:	

MERLIN	Date:
	Location:
Notes:	

EURASIAN HOBBY ▲	Date:
	Location:
Notes:	

APLOMADO FALCON	Date:
	Location:
Notes:	

▲ RARE ■ EXTINCT

Falcons

GYRFALCON	Date:
	Location:
Notes:	

PEREGRINE FALCON	Date:
	Location:
Notes:	

PRAIRIE FALCON	Date:
	Location:
Notes:	

ROSY-FACED LOVEBIRD	Date:
	Location:
Notes:	

MONK PARAKEET	Date:
	Location:
Notes:	

▲ RARE ■ EXTINCT

WHITE-WINGED PARAKEET	Date:
	Location:
Notes:	

RED-CROWNED PARROT	Date:
	Location:
Notes:	

THICK-BILLED PARROT ▲	Date:
	Location:
Notes:	

CAROLINA PARAKEET ■	Date:
	Location:
Notes:	

NANDAY PARAKEET	Date:
	Location:
Notes:	

▲ RARE   ■ EXTINCT

Parrots

NORTHERN BEARDLESS-TYRANNULET	Date:
	Location:
Notes:	

GREENISH ELAENIA ▲	Date:
	Location:
Notes:	

WHITE-CRESTED ELAENIA ▲	Date:
	Location:
Notes:	

TUFTED FLYCATCHER ▲	Date:
	Location:
Notes:	

OLIVE-SIDED FLYCATCHER	Date:
	Location:
Notes:	

▲ RARE   ■ EXTINCT

GREATER PEWEE	Date:
	Location:
Notes:	

WESTERN WOOD-PEWEE	Date:
	Location:
Notes:	

EASTERN WOOD-PEWEE	Date:
	Location:
Notes:	

CUBAN PEWEE ▲	Date:
	Location:
Notes:	

YELLOW-BELLIED FLYCATCHER	Date:
	Location:
Notes:	

▲ RARE ■ EXTINCT

Tyrant Flycatchers

ACADIAN FLYCATCHER	Date:
	Location:
Notes:	

ALDER FLYCATCHER	Date:
	Location:
Notes:	

WILLOW FLYCATCHER	Date:
	Location:
Notes:	

LEAST FLYCATCHER	Date:
	Location:
Notes:	

HAMMOND'S FLYCATCHER	Date:
	Location:
Notes:	

▲ RARE   ■ EXTINCT

GRAY FLYCATCHER	Date:
	Location:

Notes:

DUSKY FLYCATCHER	Date:
	Location:

Notes:

PACIFIC-SLOPE FLYCATCHER	Date:
	Location:

Notes:

CORDILLERAN FLYCATCHER	Date:
	Location:

Notes:

BUFF-BREASTED FLYCATCHER	Date:
	Location:

Notes:

▲ RARE ■ EXTINCT

Tyrant Flycatchers

BLACK PHOEBE	Date:
	Location:
Notes:	

EASTERN PHOEBE	Date:
	Location:
Notes:	

SAY'S PHOEBE	Date:
	Location:
Notes:	

VERMILION FLYCATCHER	Date:
	Location:
Notes:	

DUSKY-CAPPED FLYCATCHER	Date:
	Location:
Notes:	

▲ RARE ■ EXTINCT

ASH-THROATED FLYCATCHER	Date:
	Location:
Notes:	

NUTTING'S FLYCATCHER ▲	Date:
	Location:
Notes:	

GREAT CRESTED FLYCATCHER	Date:
	Location:
Notes:	

BROWN-CRESTED FLYCATCHER	Date:
	Location:
Notes:	

LA SAGRA'S FLYCATCHER ▲	Date:
	Location:
Notes:	

▲ RARE ■ EXTINCT

Tyrant Flycatchers

GREAT KISKADEE	Date:
	Location:
Notes:	

SOCIAL FLYCATCHER ▲	Date:
	Location:
Notes:	

SULPHUR-BELLIED FLYCATCHER	Date:
	Location:
Notes:	

PIRATIC FLYCATCHER ▲	Date:
	Location:
Notes:	

VARIEGATED FLYCATCHER ▲	Date:
	Location:
Notes:	

▲ RARE   ■ EXTINCT

CROWNED SLATY FLYCATCHER ▲	Date:
	Location:
Notes:	

TROPICAL KINGBIRD	Date:
	Location:
Notes:	

COUCH'S KINGBIRD	Date:
	Location:
Notes:	

CASSIN'S KINGBIRD	Date:
	Location:
Notes:	

THICK-BILLED KINGBIRD	Date:
	Location:
Notes:	

Tyrant Flycatchers

WESTERN KINGBIRD	Date:
	Location:
Notes:	

EASTERN KINGBIRD	Date:
	Location:
Notes:	

GRAY KINGBIRD	Date:
	Location:
Notes:	

LOGGERHEAD KINGBIRD ▲	Date:
	Location:
Notes:	

SCISSOR-TAILED FLYCATCHER	Date:
	Location:
Notes:	

▲ RARE ■ EXTINCT

FORK-TAILED FLYCATCHER ▲	Date:
	Location:

Notes:

MASKED TITYRA ▲	Date:
	Location:

Notes:

GRAY-COLLARED BECARD ▲	Date:
	Location:

Notes:

ROSE-THROATED BECARD	Date:
	Location:

Notes:

BROWN SHRIKE ▲	Date:
	Location:

Notes:

Shrikes

LOGGERHEAD SHRIKE	Date:
	Location:
Notes:	

NORTHERN SHRIKE	Date:
	Location:
Notes:	

WHITE-EYED VIREO	Date:
	Location:
Notes:	

THICK-BILLED VIREO ▲	Date:
	Location:
Notes:	

BELL'S VIREO	Date:
	Location:
Notes:	

▲ RARE ■ EXTINCT

BLACK-CAPPED VIREO	Date:
	Location:
Notes:	

GRAY VIREO	Date:
	Location:
Notes:	

YELLOW-THROATED VIREO	Date:
	Location:
Notes:	

PLUMBEOUS VIREO	Date:
	Location:
Notes:	

CASSIN'S VIREO	Date:
	Location:
Notes:	

Vireos

BLUE-HEADED VIREO	Date:
	Location:
Notes:	

HUTTON'S VIREO	Date:
	Location:
Notes:	

WARBLING VIREO	Date:
	Location:
Notes:	

PHILADELPHIA VIREO	Date:
	Location:
Notes:	

RED-EYED VIREO	Date:
	Location:
Notes:	

▲ RARE ■ EXTINCT

YELLOW-GREEN VIREO ▲	Date:
	Location:

Notes:

BLACK-WHISKERED VIREO	Date:
	Location:

Notes:

YUCATAN VIREO ▲	Date:
	Location:

Notes:

GRAY JAY	Date:
	Location:

Notes:

BROWN JAY ▲	Date:
	Location:

Notes:

Crows and Jays

GREEN JAY	Date:
	Location:
Notes:	

PINYON JAY	Date:
	Location:
Notes:	

STELLER'S JAY	Date:
	Location:
Notes:	

BLUE JAY	Date:
	Location:
Notes:	

FLORIDA SCRUB-JAY	Date:
	Location:
Notes:	

▲ RARE ■ EXTINCT

ISLAND SCRUB-JAY	Date:
	Location:
Notes:	

WESTERN SCRUB-JAY	Date:
	Location:
Notes:	

MEXICAN JAY	Date:
	Location:
Notes:	

BLACK-BILLED MAGPIE	Date:
	Location:
Notes:	

YELLOW-BILLED MAGPIE	Date:
	Location:
Notes:	

Crows and Jays

CLARK'S NUTCRACKER	Date:
	Location:
Notes:	

EURASIAN JACKDAW ▲	Date:
	Location:
Notes:	

AMERICAN CROW	Date:
	Location:
Notes:	

NORTHWESTERN CROW	Date:
	Location:
Notes:	

TAMAULIPAS CROW ▲	Date:
	Location:
Notes:	

▲ RARE ■ EXTINCT

FISH CROW	Date:
	Location:
Notes:	

CHIHUAHUAN RAVEN	Date:
	Location:
Notes:	

COMMON RAVEN	Date:
	Location:
Notes:	

SKY LARK	Date:
	Location:
Notes:	

HORNED LARK	Date:
	Location:
Notes:	

Larks

NORTHERN ROUGH-WINGED SWALLOW	Date:
	Location:
Notes:	

PURPLE MARTIN	Date:
	Location:
Notes:	

CUBAN MARTIN ▲	Date:
	Location:
Notes:	

GRAY-BREASTED MARTIN ▲	Date:
	Location:
Notes:	

SOUTHERN MARTIN ▲	Date:
	Location:
Notes:	

▲ RARE ■ EXTINCT

BROWN-CHESTED MARTIN ▲	Date:
	Location:
Notes:	

TREE SWALLOW	Date:
	Location:
Notes:	

MANGROVE SWALLOW ▲	Date:
	Location:
Notes:	

VIOLET-GREEN SWALLOW	Date:
	Location:
Notes:	

BAHAMA SWALLOW ▲	Date:
	Location:
Notes:	

Swallows

BANK SWALLOW	Date:
	Location:
Notes:	

BARN SWALLOW	Date:
	Location:
Notes:	

CLIFF SWALLOW	Date:
	Location:
Notes:	

CAVE SWALLOW	Date:
	Location:
Notes:	

COMMON HOUSE-MARTIN ▲	Date:
	Location:
Notes:	

▲ RARE ■ EXTINCT

CAROLINA CHICKADEE	Date:
	Location:

Notes:

BLACK-CAPPED CHICKADEE	Date:
	Location:

Notes:

MOUNTAIN CHICKADEE	Date:
	Location:

Notes:

MEXICAN CHICKADEE	Date:
	Location:

Notes:

CHESTNUT-BACKED CHICKADEE	Date:
	Location:

Notes:

▲ RARE ■ EXTINCT

Chickadees

BOREAL CHICKADEE	Date:
	Location:
Notes:	

GRAY-HEADED CHICKADEE	Date:
	Location:
Notes:	

BRIDLED TITMOUSE	Date:
	Location:
Notes:	

OAK TITMOUSE	Date:
	Location:
Notes:	

JUNIPER TITMOUSE	Date:
	Location:
Notes:	

▲ RARE ■ EXTINCT

TUFTED TITMOUSE	Date:
	Location:

Notes:

BLACK-CRESTED TITMOUSE	Date:
	Location:

Notes:

VERDIN	Date:
	Location:

Notes:

BUSHTIT	Date:
	Location:

Notes:

RED-BREASTED NUTHATCH	Date:
	Location:

Notes:

▲ RARE ■ EXTINCT

Nuthatches

WHITE-BREASTED NUTHATCH	Date:
	Location:
Notes:	

PYGMY NUTHATCH	Date:
	Location:
Notes:	

BROWN-HEADED NUTHATCH	Date:
	Location:
Notes:	

BROWN CREEPER	Date:
	Location:
Notes:	

ROCK WREN	Date:
	Location:
Notes:	

▲ RARE ■ EXTINCT

CANYON WREN	Date:
	Location:
Notes:	

HOUSE WREN	Date:
	Location:
Notes:	

PACIFIC WREN	Date:
	Location:
Notes:	

WINTER WREN	Date:
	Location:
Notes:	

SEDGE WREN	Date:
	Location:
Notes:	

Wrens

MARSH WREN	Date:
	Location:
Notes:	

CAROLINA WREN	Date:
	Location:
Notes:	

BEWICK'S WREN	Date:
	Location:
Notes:	

CACTUS WREN	Date:
	Location:
Notes:	

SINALOA WREN ▲	Date:
	Location:
Notes:	

▲ RARE ■ EXTINCT

BLUE-GRAY GNATCATCHER	Date:
	Location:

Notes:

CALIFORNIA GNATCATCHER	Date:
	Location:

Notes:

BLACK-TAILED GNATCATCHER	Date:
	Location:

Notes:

BLACK-CAPPED GNATCATCHER	Date:
	Location:

Notes:

AMERICAN DIPPER	Date:
	Location:

Notes:

Bulbul

RED-WHISKERED BULBUL	Date:
	Location:
Notes:	

GOLDEN-CROWNED KINGLET	Date:
	Location:
Notes:	

RUBY-CROWNED KINGLET	Date:
	Location:
Notes:	

WILLOW WARBLER ▲	Date:
	Location:
Notes:	

COMMON CHIFFCHAFF ▲	Date:
	Location:
Notes:	

▲ RARE ■ EXTINCT

WOOD WARBLER ▲	Date:
	Location:

Notes:

DUSKY WARBLER ▲	Date:
	Location:

Notes:

PALLAS'S LEAF WARBLER ▲	Date:
	Location:

Notes:

YELLOW-BROWED WARBLER ▲	Date:
	Location:

Notes:

ARCTIC WARBLER	Date:
	Location:

Notes:

▲ RARE ■ EXTINCT

Warblers

KAMCHATKA LEAF WARBLER ▲	Date:
	Location:
Notes:	

SEDGE WARBLER ▲	Date:
	Location:
Notes:	

BLYTH'S REED-WARBLER ▲	Date:
	Location:
Notes:	

MIDDENDORFF'S GRASSHOPPER-WARBLER ▲	Date:
	Location:
Notes:	

LANCEOLATED WARBLER ▲	Date:
	Location:
Notes:	

▲ RARE ■ EXTINCT

LESSER WHITETHROAT ▲	Date:
	Location:
Notes:	

WRENTIT	Date:
	Location:
Notes:	

SPOTTED FLYCATCHER ▲	Date:
	Location:
Notes:	

DARK-SIDED FLYCATCHER ▲	Date:
	Location:
Notes:	

ASIAN BROWN FLYCATCHER ▲	Date:
	Location:
Notes:	

▲ RARE ■ EXTINCT

Flycatchers

GRAY-STREAKED FLYCATCHER ▲	Date:
	Location:
Notes:	

RUFOUS-TAILED ROBIN ▲	Date:
	Location:
Notes:	

SIBERIAN BLUE ROBIN ▲	Date:
	Location:
Notes:	

BLUETHROAT	Date:
	Location:
Notes:	

SIBERIAN RUBYTHROAT ▲	Date:
	Location:
Notes:	

▲ RARE ■ EXTINCT

RED-FLANKED BLUETAIL ▲	Date:
	Location:

Notes:

NARCISSUS FLYCATCHER ▲	Date:
	Location:

Notes:

MUGIMAKI FLYCATCHER ▲	Date:
	Location:

Notes:

TAIGA FLYCATCHER ▲	Date:
	Location:

Notes:

COMMON REDSTART ▲	Date:
	Location:

Notes:

Flycatchers

STONECHAT ▲	Date:
	Location:
Notes:	

NORTHERN WHEATEAR	Date:
	Location:
Notes:	

EASTERN BLUEBIRD	Date:
	Location:
Notes:	

WESTERN BLUEBIRD	Date:
	Location:
Notes:	

MOUNTAIN BLUEBIRD	Date:
	Location:
Notes:	

▲ RARE ■ EXTINCT

TOWNSEND'S SOLITAIRE	Date:
	Location:

Notes:

BROWN-BACKED SOLITAIRE ▲	Date:
	Location:

Notes:

ORANGE-BILLED NIGHTINGALE-THRUSH ▲	Date:
	Location:

Notes:

BLACK-HEADED NIGHTINGALE-THRUSH ▲	Date:
	Location:

Notes:

VEERY	Date:
	Location:

Notes:

Thrushes

GRAY-CHEEKED THRUSH	Date:
	Location:
Notes:	

BICKNELL'S THRUSH	Date:
	Location:
Notes:	

SWAINSON'S THRUSH	Date:
	Location:
Notes:	

HERMIT THRUSH	Date:
	Location:
Notes:	

WOOD THRUSH	Date:
	Location:
Notes:	

▲ RARE ■ EXTINCT

EURASIAN BLACKBIRD ▲	Date:
	Location:

Notes:

EYEBROWED THRUSH ▲	Date:
	Location:

Notes:

DUSKY THRUSH ▲	Date:
	Location:

Notes:

FIELDFARE ▲	Date:
	Location:

Notes:

REDWING ▲	Date:
	Location:

Notes:

▲ RARE ■ EXTINCT

Thrushes

SONG THRUSH ▲	Date:
	Location:
Notes:	

CLAY-COLORED THRUSH	Date:
	Location:
Notes:	

WHITE-THROATED THRUSH ▲	Date:
	Location:
Notes:	

RUFOUS-BACKED ROBIN	Date:
	Location:
Notes:	

AMERICAN ROBIN	Date:
	Location:
Notes:	

▲ RARE ■ EXTINCT

RED-LEGGED THRUSH ▲	Date:
	Location:
Notes:	

VARIED THRUSH	Date:
	Location:
Notes:	

AZTEC THRUSH ▲	Date:
	Location:
Notes:	

BLUE MOCKINGBIRD ▲	Date:
	Location:
Notes:	

GRAY CATBIRD	Date:
	Location:
Notes:	

▲ RARE   ■ EXTINCT

Mockingbirds and Thrashers

CURVE-BILLED THRASHER	Date:
	Location:
Notes:	

BROWN THRASHER	Date:
	Location:
Notes:	

LONG-BILLED THRASHER	Date:
	Location:
Notes:	

BENDIRE'S THRASHER	Date:
	Location:
Notes:	

CALIFORNIA THRASHER	Date:
	Location:
Notes:	

LE CONTE'S THRASHER	Date:
	Location:

Notes:

CRISSAL THRASHER	Date:
	Location:

Notes:

SAGE THRASHER	Date:
	Location:

Notes:

BAHAMA MOCKINGBIRD ▲	Date:
	Location:

Notes:

NORTHERN MOCKINGBIRD	Date:
	Location:

Notes:

▲ RARE ■ EXTINCT

Mockingbirds and Thrashers

EUROPEAN STARLING	Date:
	Location:
Notes:	

COMMON MYNA	Date:
	Location:
Notes:	

SIBERIAN ACCENTOR ▲	Date:
	Location:
Notes:	

EASTERN YELLOW WAGTAIL	Date:
	Location:
Notes:	

CITRINE WAGTAIL ▲	Date:
	Location:
Notes:	

▲ RARE ■ EXTINCT

GRAY WAGTAIL ▲	Date:
	Location:

Notes:

WHITE WAGTAIL	Date:
	Location:

Notes:

TREE PIPIT ▲	Date:
	Location:

Notes:

OLIVE-BACKED PIPIT ▲	Date:
	Location:

Notes:

PECHORA PIPIT ▲	Date:
	Location:

Notes:

Wagtails and Pipits

RED-THROATED PIPIT ▲	Date:
	Location:
Notes:	

AMERICAN PIPIT	Date:
	Location:
Notes:	

SPRAGUE'S PIPIT	Date:
	Location:
Notes:	

BOHEMIAN WAXWING	Date:
	Location:
Notes:	

CEDAR WAXWING	Date:
	Location:
Notes:	

▲ RARE ■ EXTINCT

GRAY SILKY-FLYCATCHER ▲	Date:
	Location:

Notes:

PHAINOPEPLA	Date:
	Location:

Notes:

OLIVE WARBLER	Date:
	Location:

Notes:

LAPLAND LONGSPUR	Date:
	Location:

Notes:

CHESTNUT-COLLARED LONGSPUR	Date:
	Location:

Notes:

▲ RARE ■ EXTINCT

Longspurs

SMITH'S LONGSPUR	Date:
	Location:
Notes:	

McCOWN'S LONGSPUR	Date:
	Location:
Notes:	

SNOW BUNTING	Date:
	Location:
Notes:	

McKAY'S BUNTING	Date:
	Location:
Notes:	

OVENBIRD	Date:
	Location:
Notes:	

▲ RARE ■ EXTINCT

WORM-EATING WARBLER	Date:
	Location:

Notes:

LOUISIANA WATERTHRUSH	Date:
	Location:

Notes:

NORTHERN WATERTHRUSH	Date:
	Location:

Notes:

BACHMAN'S WARBLER ■	Date:
	Location:

Notes:

GOLDEN-WINGED WARBLER	Date:
	Location:

Notes:

Wood Warblers

BLUE-WINGED WARBLER	Date:
	Location:
Notes:	

BLACK-AND-WHITE WARBLER	Date:
	Location:
Notes:	

PROTHONOTARY WARBLER	Date:
	Location:
Notes:	

SWAINSON'S WARBLER	Date:
	Location:
Notes:	

CRESCENT-CHESTED WARBLER ▲	Date:
	Location:
Notes:	

▲ RARE ■ EXTINCT

TENNESSEE WARBLER	Date:
	Location:

Notes:

ORANGE-CROWNED WARBLER	Date:
	Location:

Notes:

COLIMA WARBLER	Date:
	Location:

Notes:

LUCY'S WARBLER	Date:
	Location:

Notes:

NASHVILLE WARBLER	Date:
	Location:

Notes:

Wood Warblers

VIRGINIA'S WARBLER	Date:
	Location:
Notes:	

CONNECTICUT WARBLER	Date:
	Location:
Notes:	

GRAY-CROWNED YELLOWTHROAT ▲	Date:
	Location:
Notes:	

MacGILLIVRAY'S WARBLER	Date:
	Location:
Notes:	

MOURNING WARBLER	Date:
	Location:
Notes:	

▲ RARE ■ EXTINCT

KENTUCKY WARBLER	Date:
	Location:

Notes:

COMMON YELLOWTHROAT	Date:
	Location:

Notes:

HOODED WARBLER	Date:
	Location:

Notes:

AMERICAN REDSTART	Date:
	Location:

Notes:

KIRTLAND'S WARBLER	Date:
	Location:

Notes:

▲ RARE ■ EXTINCT

Wood Warblers

CAPE MAY WARBLER	Date:
	Location:
Notes:	

CERULEAN WARBLER	Date:
	Location:
Notes:	

NORTHERN PARULA	Date:
	Location:
Notes:	

TROPICAL PARULA ▲	Date:
	Location:
Notes:	

MAGNOLIA WARBLER	Date:
	Location:
Notes:	

▲ RARE ■ EXTINCT

BAY-BREASTED WARBLER	Date:
	Location:
Notes:	

BLACKBURNIAN WARBLER	Date:
	Location:
Notes:	

YELLOW WARBLER	Date:
	Location:
Notes:	

CHESTNUT-SIDED WARBLER	Date:
	Location:
Notes:	

BLACKPOLL WARBLER	Date:
	Location:
Notes:	

Wood Warblers

BLACK-THROATED BLUE WARBLER	Date:
	Location:
Notes:	

PALM WARBLER	Date:
	Location:
Notes:	

PINE WARBLER	Date:
	Location:
Notes:	

YELLOW-RUMPED WARBLER	Date:
	Location:
Notes:	

YELLOW-THROATED WARBLER	Date:
	Location:
Notes:	

▲ RARE ■ EXTINCT

PRAIRIE WARBLER	Date:
	Location:

Notes:

GRACE'S WARBLER	Date:
	Location:

Notes:

BLACK-THROATED GRAY WARBLER	Date:
	Location:

Notes:

TOWNSEND'S WARBLER	Date:
	Location:

Notes:

HERMIT WARBLER	Date:
	Location:

Notes:

▲ RARE   ■ EXTINCT

Wood Warblers

GOLDEN-CHEEKED WARBLER	Date:
	Location:
Notes:	

BLACK-THROATED GREEN WARBLER	Date:
	Location:
Notes:	

FAN-TAILED WARBLER ▲	Date:
	Location:
Notes:	

RUFOUS-CAPPED WARBLER ▲	Date:
	Location:
Notes:	

GOLDEN-CROWNED WARBLER ▲	Date:
	Location:
Notes:	

▲ RARE ■ EXTINCT

CANADA WARBLER	Date:
	Location:

Notes:

WILSON'S WARBLER	Date:
	Location:

Notes:

RED-FACED WARBLER	Date:
	Location:

Notes:

PAINTED REDSTART	Date:
	Location:

Notes:

SLATE-THROATED REDSTART ▲	Date:
	Location:

Notes:

Wood Warblers

YELLOW-BREASTED CHAT	Date:
	Location:
Notes:	

WHITE-COLLARED SEEDEATER ▲	Date:
	Location:
Notes:	

BANANAQUIT ▲	Date:
	Location:
Notes:	

YELLOW-FACED GRASSQUIT ▲	Date:
	Location:
Notes:	

BLACK-FACED GRASSQUIT ▲	Date:
	Location:
Notes:	

▲ RARE ■ EXTINCT

WESTERN SPINDALIS ▲	Date:
	Location:

Notes:

RUFOUS-WINGED SPARROW	Date:
	Location:

Notes:

BOTTERI'S SPARROW	Date:
	Location:

Notes:

CASSIN'S SPARROW	Date:
	Location:

Notes:

BACHMAN'S SPARROW	Date:
	Location:

Notes:

GRASSHOPPER SPARROW	Date:
	Location:

Notes:

BAIRD'S SPARROW	Date:
	Location:

Notes:

HENSLOW'S SPARROW	Date:
	Location:

Notes:

LE CONTE'S SPARROW	Date:
	Location:

Notes:

NELSON'S SPARROW	Date:
	Location:

Notes:

▲ RARE ■ EXTINCT

SALTMARSH SPARROW	Date:
	Location:

Notes:

SEASIDE SPARROW	Date:
	Location:

Notes:

OLIVE SPARROW	Date:
	Location:

Notes:

AMERICAN TREE SPARROW	Date:
	Location:

Notes:

CHIPPING SPARROW	Date:
	Location:

Notes:

▲ RARE   ■ EXTINCT

Emberizine Sparrows

CLAY-COLORED SPARROW	Date:
	Location:
Notes:	

BLACK-CHINNED SPARROW	Date:
	Location:
Notes:	

FIELD SPARROW	Date:
	Location:
Notes:	

BREWER'S SPARROW	Date:
	Location:
Notes:	

WORTHEN'S SPARROW ▲	Date:
	Location:
Notes:	

▲ RARE ■ EXTINCT

BLACK-THROATED SPARROW	Date:
	Location:

Notes:

FIVE-STRIPED SPARROW	Date:
	Location:

Notes:

LARK SPARROW	Date:
	Location:

Notes:

LARK BUNTING	Date:
	Location:

Notes:

FOX SPARROW	Date:
	Location:

Notes:

Emberizine Sparrows

DARK-EYED JUNCO	Date:
	Location:
Notes:	

YELLOW-EYED JUNCO	Date:
	Location:
Notes:	

WHITE-CROWNED SPARROW	Date:
	Location:
Notes:	

GOLDEN-CROWNED SPARROW	Date:
	Location:
Notes:	

HARRIS'S SPARROW	Date:
	Location:
Notes:	

▲ RARE ■ EXTINCT

WHITE-THROATED SPARROW	Date:
	Location:

Notes:

SAGEBRUSH SPARROW	Date:
	Location:

Notes:

BELL'S SPARROW	Date:
	Location:

Notes:

VESPER SPARROW	Date:
	Location:

Notes:

SAVANNAH SPARROW	Date:
	Location:

Notes:

Emberizine Sparrows

SONG SPARROW	Date:
	Location:
Notes:	

LINCOLN'S SPARROW	Date:
	Location:
Notes:	

SWAMP SPARROW	Date:
	Location:
Notes:	

CANYON TOWHEE	Date:
	Location:
Notes:	

ABERT'S TOWHEE	Date:
	Location:
Notes:	

▲ RARE ■ EXTINCT

CALIFORNIA TOWHEE	Date:
	Location:
Notes:	

RUFOUS-CROWNED SPARROW	Date:
	Location:
Notes:	

GREEN-TAILED TOWHEE	Date:
	Location:
Notes:	

SPOTTED TOWHEE	Date:
	Location:
Notes:	

EASTERN TOWHEE	Date:
	Location:
Notes:	

▲ RARE ■ EXTINCT

Emberizine Sparrows

PINE BUNTING ▲	Date:
	Location:
Notes:	

YELLOW-BROWED BUNTING ▲	Date:
	Location:
Notes:	

LITTLE BUNTING ▲	Date:
	Location:
Notes:	

RUSTIC BUNTING ▲	Date:
	Location:
Notes:	

YELLOW-THROATED BUNTING ▲	Date:
	Location:
Notes:	

▲ RARE   ■ EXTINCT

YELLOW-BREASTED BUNTING ▲	Date:
	Location:
Notes:	

GRAY BUNTING ▲	Date:
	Location:
Notes:	

PALLAS'S BUNTING ▲	Date:
	Location:
Notes:	

REED BUNTING ▲	Date:
	Location:
Notes:	

HEPATIC TANAGER	Date:
	Location:
Notes:	

▲ RARE   ■ EXTINCT

Emberizine Sparrows

SUMMER TANAGER	Date:
	Location:
Notes:	

SCARLET TANAGER	Date:
	Location:
Notes:	

WESTERN TANAGER	Date:
	Location:
Notes:	

FLAME-COLORED TANAGER ▲	Date:
	Location:
Notes:	

CRIMSON-COLLARED GROSBEAK ▲	Date:
	Location:
Notes:	

▲ RARE   ■ EXTINCT

NORTHERN CARDINAL	Date:
	Location:

Notes:

PYRRHULOXIA	Date:
	Location:

Notes:

YELLOW GROSBEAK ▲	Date:
	Location:

Notes:

ROSE-BREASTED GROSBEAK	Date:
	Location:

Notes:

BLACK-HEADED GROSBEAK	Date:
	Location:

Notes:

▲ RARE ■ EXTINCT

Cardinals

BLUE BUNTING ▲	Date:
	Location:
Notes:	

BLUE GROSBEAK	Date:
	Location:
Notes:	

LAZULI BUNTING	Date:
	Location:
Notes:	

INDIGO BUNTING	Date:
	Location:
Notes:	

VARIED BUNTING	Date:
	Location:
Notes:	

▲ RARE ■ EXTINCT

PAINTED BUNTING	Date:
	Location:
Notes:	

DICKCISSEL	Date:
	Location:
Notes:	

BOBOLINK	Date:
	Location:
Notes:	

RED-WINGED BLACKBIRD	Date:
	Location:
Notes.	

TRICOLORED BLACKBIRD	Date:
	Location:
Notes:	

Orioles and Blackbirds

TAWNY-SHOULDERED BLACKBIRD ▲	Date:
	Location:
Notes:	

WESTERN MEADOWLARK	Date:
	Location:
Notes:	

EASTERN MEADOWLARK	Date:
	Location:
Notes:	

YELLOW-HEADED BLACKBIRD	Date:
	Location:
Notes:	

RUSTY BLACKBIRD	Date:
	Location:
Notes:	

▲ RARE ■ EXTINCT

BREWER'S BLACKBIRD	Date:
	Location:

Notes:

COMMON GRACKLE	Date:
	Location:

Notes:

BOAT-TAILED GRACKLE	Date:
	Location:

Notes:

GREAT-TAILED GRACKLE	Date:
	Location:

Notes:

SHINY COWBIRD ▲	Date:
	Location:

Notes:

Orioles and Blackbirds

BRONZED COWBIRD	Date:
	Location:
Notes:	

BROWN-HEADED COWBIRD	Date:
	Location:
Notes:	

BLACK-VENTED ORIOLE ▲	Date:
	Location:
Notes:	

ORCHARD ORIOLE	Date:
	Location:
Notes:	

HOODED ORIOLE	Date:
	Location:
Notes:	

▲ RARE ■ EXTINCT

STREAK-BACKED ORIOLE ▲	Date:
	Location:

Notes:

BULLOCK'S ORIOLE	Date:
	Location:

Notes:

SPOT-BREASTED ORIOLE	Date:
	Location:

Notes:

ALTAMIRA ORIOLE	Date:
	Location:

Notes:

AUDUBON'S ORIOLE	Date:
	Location:

Notes:

Orioles and Blackbirds

BALTIMORE ORIOLE	Date:
	Location:
Notes:	

SCOTT'S ORIOLE	Date:
	Location:
Notes:	

COMMON CHAFFINCH ▲	Date:
	Location:
Notes:	

BRAMBLING ▲	Date:
	Location:
Notes:	

ASIAN ROSY-FINCH ▲	Date:
	Location:
Notes:	

▲ RARE ■ EXTINCT

GRAY-CROWNED ROSY-FINCH	Date:
	Location:

Notes:

BLACK ROSY-FINCH	Date:
	Location:

Notes:

BROWN-CAPPED ROSY-FINCH	Date:
	Location:

Notes:

PINE GROSBEAK	Date:
	Location:

Notes:

EURASIAN BULLFINCH ▲	Date:
	Location:

Notes:

▲ RARE ■ EXTINCT

Finches

HOUSE FINCH	Date:
	Location:
Notes:	

PURPLE FINCH	Date:
	Location:
Notes:	

CASSIN'S FINCH	Date:
	Location:
Notes:	

COMMON ROSEFINCH ▲	Date:
	Location:
Notes:	

PALLAS'S ROSEFINCH ▲	Date:
	Location:
Notes:	

▲ RARE   ■ EXTINCT

ORIENTAL GREENFINCH ▲	Date:
	Location:

Notes:

RED CROSSBILL	Date:
	Location:

Notes:

WHITE-WINGED CROSSBILL	Date:
	Location:

Notes:

COMMON REDPOLL	Date:
	Location:

Notes:

HOARY REDPOLL	Date:
	Location:

Notes:

Finches

EURASIAN SISKIN ▲	Date:
	Location:
Notes:	

PINE SISKIN	Date:
	Location:
Notes:	

LESSER GOLDFINCH	Date:
	Location:
Notes:	

LAWRENCE'S GOLDFINCH	Date:
	Location:
Notes:	

AMERICAN GOLDFINCH	Date:
	Location:
Notes:	

▲ RARE ■ EXTINCT

EVENING GROSBEAK	Date:
	Location:

Notes:

HAWFINCH ▲	Date:
	Location:

Notes:

HOUSE SPARROW	Date:
	Location:

Notes:

EURASIAN TREE SPARROW	Date:
	Location:

Notes:

SCALY-BREASTED MUNIA	Date:
	Location:

Notes:

▲ RARE ■ EXTINCT

NON-ESTABLISHED EXOTICS

Non-established Exotics

SWAN GOOSE	Date:
	Location:
Notes:	

BAR-HEADED GOOSE	Date:
	Location:
Notes:	

BLACK SWAN	Date:
	Location:
Notes:	

RUDDY SHELDUCK	Date:
	Location:
Notes:	

COMMON SHELDUCK	Date:
	Location:
Notes:	

RINGED TEAL	Date:
	Location:

Notes:

MANDARIN DUCK	Date:
	Location:

Notes:

RED-CRESTED POCHARD	Date:
	Location:

Notes:

ROSY-BILLED POCHARD	Date:
	Location:

Notes:

HELMETED GUINEAFOWL	Date:
	Location:

Notes:

Non-established Exotics

INDIAN PEAFOWL	Date:
	Location:
Notes:	

RED JUNGLEFOWL	Date:
	Location:
Notes:	

GOLDEN PHEASANT	Date:
	Location:
Notes:	

CHILEAN FLAMINGO	Date:
	Location:
Notes:	

GREATER FLAMINGO	Date:
	Location:
Notes:	

LESSER FLAMINGO	Date:
	Location:
Notes:	

HERALD PETREL	Date:
	Location:
Notes:	

AFRICAN COLLARED-DOVE	Date:
	Location:
Notes:	

SULPHUR-CRESTED COCKATOO	Date:
	Location:
Notes:	

COCKATIEL	Date:
	Location:
Notes:	

▲ RARE ■ EXTINCT

Non-established Exotics

ROSE-RINGED PARAKEET	Date:
	Location:
Notes:	

BUDGERIGAR	Date:
	Location:
Notes:	

YELLOW-CHEVRONED PARAKEET	Date:
	Location:
Notes:	

LILAC-CROWNED PARROT	Date:
	Location:
Notes:	

RED-LORED PARROT	Date:
	Location:
Notes:	

▲ RARE ■ EXTINCT

YELLOW-NAPED PARROT	Date:
	Location:

Notes:

YELLOW-HEADED PARROT	Date:
	Location:

Notes:

YELLOW-CROWNED PARROT	Date:
	Location:

Notes:

BLUE-FRONTED PARROT	Date:
	Location:

Notes:

WHITE-FRONTED PARROT	Date:
	Location:

Notes:

▲ RARE ■ EXTINCT

Non-established Exotics

MEALY PARROT	Date:
	Location:
Notes:	

ORANGE-WINGED PARROT	Date:
	Location:
Notes:	

DUSKY-HEADED PARAKEET	Date:
	Location:
Notes:	

BLUE-AND-YELLOW MACAW	Date:
	Location:
Notes:	

CHESTNUT-FRONTED MACAW	Date:
	Location:
Notes:	

▲ RARE ■ EXTINCT

BLUE-CROWNED PARAKEET	Date:
	Location:
Notes:	

MITRED PARAKEET	Date:
	Location:
Notes:	

RED-MASKED PARAKEET	Date:
	Location:
Notes:	

WHITE-EYED PARAKEET	Date:
	Location:
Notes:	

GREEN PARAKEET	Date:
	Location:
Notes:	

▲ RARE   ■ EXTINCT

BLACK-THROATED MAGPIE-JAY	Date:
	Location:
Notes:	

HOUSE CROW	Date:
	Location:
Notes:	

HOODED CROW	Date:
	Location:
Notes:	

EURASIAN BLUE TIT	Date:
	Location:
Notes:	

GREAT TIT	Date:
	Location:
Notes:	

RED-VENTED BULBUL	Date:
	Location:

Notes:

JAPANESE WHITE-EYE	Date:
	Location:

Notes:

HILL MYNA	Date:
	Location:

Notes:

CRESTED MYNA	Date:
	Location:

Notes:

RED-CRESTED CARDINAL	Date:
	Location:

Notes:

▲ RARE ■ EXTINCT

EUROPEAN GOLDFINCH	Date:
	Location:
Notes:	

YELLOW-FRONTED CANARY	Date:
	Location:
Notes:	

ORANGE BISHOP	Date:
	Location:
Notes:	

ORANGE-CHEEKED WAXBILL	Date:
	Location:
Notes:	

BRONZE MANNIKIN	Date:
	Location:
Notes:	

TRICOLORED MUNIA	Date:
	Location:

Notes:

JAVA SPARROW	Date:
	Location:

Notes:

PIN-TAILED WHYDAH	Date:
	Location:

Notes:

	Date:
	Location:

Notes:

	Date:
	Location:

Notes:

▲ RARE ■ EXTINCT

	Date:
	Location:
Notes:	

	Date:
	Location:
Notes:	

	Date:
	Location:
Notes:	

	Date:
	Location:
Notes:	

	Date:
	Location:
Notes:	

▲ RARE ■ EXTINCT

	Date:
	Location:
Notes:	

	Date:
	Location:
Notes:	

	Date:
	Location:
Notes:	

	Date:
	Location:
Notes:	

	Date:
	Location:
Notes:	

▲ RARE ■ EXTINCT   219

	Date:
	Location:
Notes:	

	Date:
	Location:
Notes:	

	Date:
	Location:
Notes:	

	Date:
	Location:
Notes:	

	Date:
	Location:
Notes:	

▲ RARE ■ EXTINCT

	Date:
	Location:
Notes:	

	Date:
	Location:
Notes:	

	Date:
	Location:
Notes:	

	Date:
	Location:
Notes:	

	Date:
	Location:
Notes:	

▲ RARE ■ EXTINCT

	Date:
	Location:

Notes:

	Date:
	Location:

Notes:

	Date:
	Location:

Notes:

	Date:
	Location:

Notes:

	Date:
	Location:

Notes:

▲ RARE ■ EXTINCT

	Date:
	Location:
Notes:	

	Date:
	Location:
Notes:	

	Date:
	Location:
Notes:	

	Date:
	Location:
Notes:	

	Date:
	Location:
Notes:	

						DUCKS, GEESE, AND SWANS
						Black-bellied Whistling-Duck
						Fulvous Whistling-Duck
						Taiga Bean-Goose ▲
						Tundra Bean-Goose ▲
						Pink-footed Goose ▲
						Greater White-fronted Goose
						Lesser White-fronted Goose ▲
						Graylag Goose
						Emperor Goose
						Snow Goose
						Ross's Goose
						Brant
						Barnacle Goose ▲
						Cackling Goose
						Canada Goose
						Mute Swan
						Trumpeter Swan
						Tundra Swan
						Whooper Swan ▲
						Egyptian Goose
						Muscovy Duck
						Wood Duck
						Gadwall
						Falcated Duck ▲
						Eurasian Wigeon
						American Wigeon
						American Black Duck
						Mallard
						Mottled Duck
						Eastern Spot-billed Duck ▲
						Blue-winged Teal

▲ RARE   ■ EXTINCT

						Cinnamon Teal
						Northern Shoveler
						White-cheeked Pintail ▲
						Northern Pintail
						Garganey ▲
						Baikal Teal ▲
						Green-winged Teal
						Canvasback
						Redhead
						Common Pochard ▲
						Ring-necked Duck
						Tufted Duck ▲
						Greater Scaup
						Lesser Scaup
						Steller's Eider
						Spectacled Eider
						King Eider
						Common Eider
						Harlequin Duck
						Labrador Duck ■
						Surf Scoter
						White-winged Scoter
						Common Scoter ▲
						Black Scoter
						Long-tailed Duck
						Bufflehead
						Common Goldeneye
						Barrow's Goldeneye
						Smew ▲
						Hooded Merganser
						Common Merganser
						Red-breasted Merganser

▲ RARE ■ EXTINCT

						Masked Duck ▲
						Ruddy Duck
CHACHALACA						
						Plain Chachalaca
QUAIL						
						Mountain Quail
						Scaled Quail
						California Quail
						Gambel's Quail
						Northern Bobwhite
						Montezuma Quail
PHEASANTS						
						Chukar
						Himalayan Snowcock
						Ring-necked Pheasant
						Gray Partridge
						Ruffed Grouse
						Greater Sage-Grouse
						Gunnison Sage-Grouse
						Spruce Grouse
						Willow Ptarmigan
						Rock Ptarmigan
						White-tailed Ptarmigan
						Dusky Grouse
						Sooty Grouse
						Sharp-tailed Grouse
						Greater Prairie-Chicken
						Lesser Prairie-Chicken
						Wild Turkey
LOONS						
						Red-throated Loon
						Arctic Loon

▲ RARE ■ EXTINCT

						Pacific Loon
						Common Loon
						Yellow-billed Loon
						GREBES
						Least Grebe
						Pied-billed Grebe
						Horned Grebe
						Red-necked Grebe
						Eared Grebe
						Western Grebe
						Clark's Grebe
						FLAMINGOS
						American Flamingo ▲
						ALBATROSSES
						Yellow-nosed Albatross ▲
						White-capped Albatross ▲
						Salvin's Albatross ▲
						Black-browed Albatross ▲
						Light-mantled Albatross ▲
						Wandering Albatross ▲
						Laysan Albatross
						Black-footed Albatross
						Short-tailed Albatross ▲
						SHEARWATERS AND PETRELS
						Northern Fulmar
						Great-winged Petrel ▲
						Trindade Petrel ▲
						Murphy's Petrel ▲
						Providence Petrel ▲
						Zino's Petrel ▲
						Fea's Petrel ▲
						Mottled Petrel ▲

▲ RARE ■ EXTINCT

CHECKLIST

							Bermuda Petrel ▲
							Black-capped Petrel
							Hawaiian Petrel ▲
							Cook's Petrel ▲
							Stejneger's Petrel ▲
							Bulwer's Petrel ▲
							White-chinned Petrel ▲
							Parkinson's Petrel ▲
							Streaked Shearwater ▲
							Cory's Shearwater
							Cape Verde Shearwater ▲
							Pink-footed Shearwater
							Flesh-footed Shearwater
							Great Shearwater
							Wedge-tailed Shearwater ▲
							Buller's Shearwater
							Sooty Shearwater
							Short-tailed Shearwater
							Manx Shearwater
							Newell's Shearwater ▲
							Black-vented Shearwater
							Barolo Shearwater ▲
							Audubon's Shearwater
							Wilson's Storm-Petrel
							White-faced Storm-Petrel ▲
							European Storm-Petrel ▲
							Black-bellied Storm-Petrel ▲
							Fork-tailed Storm-Petrel
							Ringed Storm-Petrel ▲
							Leach's Storm-Petrel
							Swinhoe's Storm-Petrel ▲
							Ashy Storm-Petrel

▲ RARE ■ EXTINCT

CHECKLIST

						Band-rumped Storm-Petrel
						Wedge-rumped Storm-Petrel ▲
						Black Storm-Petrel
						Tristram's Storm-Petrel ▲
						Least Storm-Petrel
TROPICBIRDS						
						White-tailed Tropicbird ▲
						Red-billed Tropicbird ▲
						Red-tailed Tropicbird ▲
WOOD STORK AND JABIRU						
						Jabiru
						Wood Stork
FRIGATEBIRDS						
						Lesser Frigatebird ▲
						Magnificent Frigatebird
						Great Frigatebird ▲
BOOBIES AND GANNETS						
						Masked Booby
						Blue-footed Booby ▲
						Brown Booby
						Red-footed Booby ▲
						Northern Gannet
CORMORANTS						
						Brandt's Cormorant
						Neotropic Cormorant
						Double-crested Cormorant
						Great Cormorant
						Red-faced Cormorant
						Pelagic Cormorant
ANHINGA						
						Anhinga

▲ RARE   ■ EXTINCT

PELICANS						
						American White Pelican
						Brown Pelican
BITTERNS, HERONS, AND EGRETS						
						American Bittern
						Yellow Bittern ▲
						Least Bittern
						Bare-throated Tiger-Heron ▲
						Great Blue Heron
						Gray Heron ▲
						Great Egret
						Intermediate Egret ▲
						Chinese Egret ▲
						Little Egret ▲
						Western Reef-Heron ▲
						Snowy Egret
						Little Blue Heron
						Tricolored Heron
						Reddish Egret
						Cattle Egret
						Chinese Pond-Heron ▲
						Green Heron
						Black-crowned Night-Heron
						Yellow-crowned Night-Heron
IBISES AND ROSEATE SPOONBILL						
						White Ibis
						Scarlet Ibis ▲
						Glossy Ibis
						White-faced Ibis
						Roseate Spoonbill
VULTURES AND CONDOR						
						Black Vulture

▲ RARE ■ EXTINCT

CHECKLIST

						Turkey Vulture
						California Condor
						OSPREY
						Osprey
						HAWKS AND EAGLES
						White-tailed Kite
						Hook-billed Kite
						Swallow-tailed Kite
						Golden Eagle
						Snail Kite
						Double-toothed Kite ▲
						Mississippi Kite
						Northern Harrier
						Sharp-shinned Hawk
						Cooper's Hawk
						Northern Goshawk
						Bald Eagle
						White-tailed Eagle ▲
						Steller's Sea-Eagle ▲
						Crane Hawk ▲
						Common Black Hawk
						Roadside Hawk ▲
						Harris's Hawk
						White-tailed Hawk
						Gray Hawk
						Red-shouldered Hawk
						Broad-winged Hawk
						Short-tailed Hawk
						Swainson's Hawk
						Zone-tailed Hawk
						Red-tailed Hawk
						Rough-legged Hawk

▲ RARE ■ EXTINCT

						Ferruginous Hawk
						RAILS AND COOTS
						Yellow Rail
						Black Rail
						Corn Crake ▲
						Ridgway's Rail
						King Rail
						Clapper Rail
						Virginia Rail
						Rufous-necked Wood-Rail ▲
						Sora
						Paint-billed Crake ▲
						Spotted Rail ▲
						Purple Gallinule
						Purple Swamphen
						Common Moorhen ▲
						Common Gallinule
						Eurasian Coot ▲
						American Coot
						Sungrebe ▲
						LIMPKIN
						Limpkin
						CRANES
						Sandhill Crane
						Common Crane ▲
						Whooping Crane
						Double-striped Thick-knee ▲
						AVOCETS AND STILTS
						Black-winged Stilt ▲
						Black-necked Stilt
						American Avocet

						OYSTERCATCHERS
						Eurasian Oystercatcher ▲
						American Oystercatcher
						Black Oystercatcher
						PLOVERS
						Black-bellied Plover
						European Golden-Plover ▲
						American Golden-Plover
						Pacific Golden-Plover
						Northern Lapwing ▲
						Lesser Sand-Plover ▲
						Greater Sand-Plover ▲
						Collared Plover ▲
						Snowy Plover
						Wilson's Plover
						Common Ringed Plover
						Semipalmated Plover
						Piping Plover
						Little Ringed Plover ▲
						Killdeer
						Mountain Plover
						Eurasian Dotterel ▲
						NORTHERN JACANA
						Northern Jacana ▲
						SANDPIPERS
						Terek Sandpiper ▲
						Common Sandpiper ▲
						Spotted Sandpiper
						Green Sandpiper ▲
						Solitary Sandpiper
						Gray-tailed Tattler ▲
						Wandering Tattler

▲ RARE ■ EXTINCT

						Spotted Redshank ▲
						Greater Yellowlegs
						Common Greenshank ▲
						Willet
						Lesser Yellowlegs
						Marsh Sandpiper ▲
						Wood Sandpiper ▲
						Common Redshank ▲
						Upland Sandpiper
						Little Curlew ▲
						Eskimo Curlew ■
						Whimbrel
						Bristle-thighed Curlew
						Far Eastern Curlew ▲
						Slender-billed Curlew ▲
						Eurasian Curlew ▲
						Long-billed Curlew
						Black-tailed Godwit ▲
						Hudsonian Godwit
						Bar-tailed Godwit
						Marbled Godwit
						Ruddy Turnstone
						Black Turnstone
						Great Knot ▲
						Red Knot
						Surfbird
						Ruff ▲
						Broad-billed Sandpiper ▲
						Sharp-tailed Sandpiper ▲
						Stilt Sandpiper
						Curlew Sandpiper ▲
						Temminck's Stint ▲

▲ RARE ■ EXTINCT

							Long-toed Stint ▲
							Spoon-billed Sandpiper ▲
							Red-necked Stint ▲
							Sanderling
							Dunlin
							Rock Sandpiper
							Purple Sandpiper
							Baird's Sandpiper
							Little Stint ▲
							Least Sandpiper
							White-rumped Sandpiper
							Buff-breasted Sandpiper
							Pectoral Sandpiper
							Semipalmated Sandpiper
							Western Sandpiper
							Short-billed Dowitcher
							Long-billed Dowitcher
							Jack Snipe ▲
							Solitary Snipe ▲
							Wilson's Snipe
							Common Snipe ▲
							Pin-tailed Snipe ▲
							Eurasian Woodcock ▲
							American Woodcock
							Wilson's Phalarope
							Red-necked Phalarope
							Red Phalarope
							Oriental Pratincole ▲
							SKUAS AND JAEGERS
							Great Skua
							South Polar Skua
							Pomarine Jaeger

▲ RARE ■ EXTINCT

CHECKLIST

						Parasitic Jaeger
						Long-tailed Jaeger
ALCIDS						
						Dovekie
						Common Murre
						Thick-billed Murre
						Razorbill
						Great Auk ■
						Black Guillemot
						Pigeon Guillemot
						Long-billed Murrelet ▲
						Marbled Murrelet
						Kittlitz's Murrelet
						Scripps's Murrelet
						Guadalupe Murrelet ▲
						Craveri's Murrelet ▲
						Ancient Murrelet
						Cassin's Auklet
						Parakeet Auklet
						Least Auklet
						Whiskered Auklet
						Crested Auklet
						Rhinoceros Auklet
						Atlantic Puffin
						Horned Puffin
						Tufted Puffin
GULLS, TERNS, AND SKIMMER						
						Swallow-tailed Gull ▲
						Black-legged Kittiwake
						Red-legged Kittiwake
						Ivory Gull
						Sabine's Gull

▲ RARE   ■ EXTINCT

CHECKLIST

						Bonaparte's Gull
						Gray-hooded Gull ▲
						Black-headed Gull
						Little Gull
						Ross's Gull
						Laughing Gull
						Franklin's Gull
						Belcher's Gull ▲
						Black-tailed Gull ▲
						Heermann's Gull
						Mew Gull
						Ring-billed Gull
						Western Gull
						Yellow-footed Gull
						California Gull
						Herring Gull
						Yellow-legged Gull ▲
						Thayer's Gull
						Iceland Gull
						Lesser Black-backed Gull
						Slaty-backed Gull
						Glaucous-winged Gull
						Glaucous Gull
						Great Black-backed Gull
						Kelp Gull ▲
						Brown Noddy
						Black Noddy ▲
						Sooty Tern
						Bridled Tern
						Aleutian Tern
						Least Tern
						Large-billed Tern ▲

▲ RARE   ■ EXTINCT

CHECKLIST

							Gull-billed Tern
							Caspian Tern
							Black Tern
							White-winged Tern ▲
							Whiskered Tern ▲
							Roseate Tern
							Common Tern
							Arctic Tern
							Forster's Tern
							Royal Tern
							Sandwich Tern
							Elegant Tern
							Black Skimmer
							PIGEONS AND DOVES
							Rock Pigeon
							Scaly-naped Pigeon ▲
							White-crowned Pigeon
							Red-billed Pigeon
							Band-tailed Pigeon
							Passenger Pigeon ■
							European Turtle-Dove ▲
							Oriental Turtle-Dove ▲
							Eurasian Collared-Dove
							African Collared-Dove
							Spotted Dove
							Inca Dove
							Common Ground-Dove
							Ruddy Ground-Dove
							Ruddy Quail-Dove ▲
							Key West Quail-Dove ▲
							White-tipped Dove
							White-winged Dove

▲ RARE ■ EXTINCT

						Zenaida Dove ▲
						Mourning Dove
					CUCKOOS	
						Common Cuckoo ▲
						Oriental Cuckoo ▲
						Yellow-billed Cuckoo
						Mangrove Cuckoo
						Black-billed Cuckoo
						Greater Roadrunner
						Smooth-billed Ani ▲
						Groove-billed Ani
					BARN OWL	
						Barn Owl
					OWLS	
						Oriental Scops-Owl ▲
						Flammulated Owl
						Western Screech-Owl
						Eastern Screech-Owl
						Whiskered Screech-Owl
						Great Horned Owl
						Snowy Owl
						Northern Hawk Owl
						Northern Pygmy-Owl
						Ferruginous Pygmy-Owl
						Elf Owl
						Burrowing Owl
						Mottled Owl ▲
						Spotted Owl
						Barred Owl
						Great Gray Owl
						Long-eared Owl
						Stygian Owl ▲

▲ RARE ■ EXTINCT

CHECKLIST

						Short-eared Owl
						Boreal Owl
						Northern Saw-whet Owl
						Northern Boobook ▲
						NIGHTJARS
						Lesser Nighthawk
						Common Nighthawk
						Antillean Nighthawk
						Common Pauraque
						Common Poorwill
						Chuck-will's-widow
						Buff-collared Nightjar
						Eastern Whip-poor-will
						Mexican Whip-poor-will
						Gray Nightjar ▲
						SWIFTS
						Black Swift
						White-collared Swift ▲
						Chimney Swift
						Vaux's Swift
						White-throated Needletail ▲
						Common Swift ▲
						Fork-tailed Swift ▲
						White-throated Swift
						Antillean Palm-Swift ▲
						HUMMINGBIRDS
						Green Violetear ▲
						Green-breasted Mango ▲
						Magnificent Hummingbird
						Plain-capped Starthroat ▲
						Blue-throated Hummingbird
						Lucifer Hummingbird

▲ RARE   ■ EXTINCT

							Bahama Woodstar ▲
							Ruby-throated Hummingbird
							Black-chinned Hummingbird
							Anna's Hummingbird
							Costa's Hummingbird
							Bumblebee Hummingbird ▲
							Broad-tailed Hummingbird
							Rufous Hummingbird
							Allen's Hummingbird
							Calliope Hummingbird
							Broad-billed Hummingbird
							Berylline Hummingbird ▲
							Buff-bellied Hummingbird
							Cinnamon Hummingbird ▲
							Violet-crowned Hummingbird
							White-eared Hummingbird
							Xantus's Hummingbird ▲
							TROGONS
							Eared Quetzal ▲
							Elegant Trogon
							Eurasian Hoopoe ▲
							KINGFISHERS
							Ringed Kingfisher
							Belted Kingfisher
							Amazon Kingfisher ▲
							Green Kingfisher
							WOODPECKERS
							Eurasian Wryneck ▲
							Lewis's Woodpecker
							Red-headed Woodpecker
							Acorn Woodpecker
							Gila Woodpecker

▲ RARE ■ EXTINCT

						Golden-fronted Woodpecker
						Red-bellied Woodpecker
						Williamson's Sapsucker
						Yellow-bellied Sapsucker
						Red-naped Sapsucker
						Red-breasted Sapsucker
						Great Spotted Woodpecker ▲
						Ladder-backed Woodpecker
						Nuttall's Woodpecker
						Downy Woodpecker
						Hairy Woodpecker
						Arizona Woodpecker
						Red-cockaded Woodpecker
						White-headed Woodpecker
						American Three-toed Woodpecker
						Black-backed Woodpecker
						Northern Flicker
						Gilded Flicker
						Pileated Woodpecker
						Ivory-billed Woodpecker ■
						FALCONS
						Collared Forest-Falcon ▲
						Crested Caracara
						Eurasian Kestrel ▲
						American Kestrel
						Red-footed Falcon ▲
						Merlin
						Eurasian Hobby ▲
						Aplomado Falcon
						Gyrfalcon
						Peregrine Falcon
						Prairie Falcon

▲ RARE ■ EXTINCT

CHECKLIST

						PARROTS
						Rosy-faced Lovebird
						Monk Parakeet
						White-winged Parakeet
						Red-crowned Parrot
						Thick-billed Parrot ▲
						Carolina Parakeet ■
						Nanday Parakeet
						TYRANT FLYCATCHERS
						Northern Beardless-Tyrannulet
						Greenish Elaenia ▲
						White-crested Elaenia ▲
						Tufted Flycatcher ▲
						Olive-sided Flycatcher
						Greater Pewee
						Western Wood-Pewee
						Eastern Wood-Pewee
						Cuban Pewee ▲
						Yellow-bellied Flycatcher
						Acadian Flycatcher
						Alder Flycatcher
						Willow Flycatcher
						Least Flycatcher
						Hammond's Flycatcher
						Gray Flycatcher
						Dusky Flycatcher
						Pacific-slope Flycatcher
						Cordilleran Flycatcher
						Buff-breasted Flycatcher
						Black Phoebe
						Eastern Phoebe
						Say's Phoebe

▲ RARE   ■ EXTINCT

							Vermilion Flycatcher
							Dusky-capped Flycatcher
							Ash-throated Flycatcher
							Nutting's Flycatcher ▲
							Great Crested Flycatcher
							Brown-crested Flycatcher
							La Sagra's Flycatcher ▲
							Great Kiskadee
							Social Flycatcher ▲
							Sulphur-bellied Flycatcher
							Piratic Flycatcher ▲
							Variegated Flycatcher ▲
							Crowned Slaty Flycatcher ▲
							Tropical Kingbird
							Couch's Kingbird
							Cassin's Kingbird
							Thick-billed Kingbird
							Western Kingbird
							Eastern Kingbird
							Gray Kingbird
							Loggerhead Kingbird ▲
							Scissor-tailed Flycatcher
							Fork-tailed Flycatcher ▲
							Masked Tityra ▲
							BECARD
							Gray-collared Becard ▲
							Rose-throated Becard
							SHRIKES
							Brown Shrike ▲
							Loggerhead Shrike
							Northern Shrike

						VIREOS
						White-eyed Vireo
						Thick-billed Vireo ▲
						Bell's Vireo
						Black-capped Vireo
						Gray Vireo
						Yellow-throated Vireo
						Plumbeous Vireo
						Cassin's Vireo
						Blue-headed Vireo
						Hutton's Vireo
						Warbling Vireo
						Philadelphia Vireo
						Red-eyed Vireo
						Yellow-green Vireo ▲
						Black-whiskered Vireo
						Yucatan Vireo ▲
						CROWS AND JAYS
						Gray Jay
						Brown Jay ▲
						Green Jay
						Pinyon Jay
						Steller's Jay
						Blue Jay
						Florida Scrub-Jay
						Island Scrub-Jay
						Western Scrub-Jay
						Mexican Jay
						Black-billed Magpie
						Yellow-billed Magpie
						Clark's Nutcracker

▲ RARE ■ EXTINCT

							Eurasian Jackdaw ▲
							American Crow
							Northwestern Crow
							Tamaulipas Crow ▲
							Fish Crow
							Chihuahuan Raven
							Common Raven
							LARKS
							Sky Lark
							Horned Lark
							SWALLOWS
							Northern Rough-winged Swallow
							Purple Martin
							Cuban Martin ▲
							Gray-breasted Martin ▲
							Southern Martin ▲
							Brown-chested Martin ▲
							Tree Swallow
							Mangrove Swallow ▲
							Violet-green Swallow
							Bahama Swallow ▲
							Bank Swallow
							Barn Swallow
							Cliff Swallow
							Cave Swallow
							Common House-Martin ▲
							CHICKADEES
							Carolina Chickadee
							Black-capped Chickadee
							Mountain Chickadee
							Mexican Chickadee
							Chestnut-backed Chickadee

▲ RARE ■ EXTINCT

							Boreal Chickadee
							Gray-headed Chickadee
							Bridled Titmouse
							Oak Titmouse
							Juniper Titmouse
							Tufted Titmouse
							Black-crested Titmouse
						VERDIN	
							Verdin
						BUSHTIT	
							Bushtit
						NUTHATCHES	
							Red-breasted Nuthatch
							White-breasted Nuthatch
							Pygmy Nuthatch
							Brown-headed Nuthatch
						CREEPER	
							Brown Creeper
						WRENS	
							Rock Wren
							Canyon Wren
							House Wren
							Pacific Wren
							Winter Wren
							Sedge Wren
							Marsh Wren
							Carolina Wren
							Bewick's Wren
							Cactus Wren
							Sinaloa Wren ▲
						GNATCATCHERS	
							Blue-gray Gnatcatcher

▲ RARE ■ EXTINCT

						California Gnatcatcher
						Black-tailed Gnatcatcher
						Black-capped Gnatcatcher
						DIPPER
						American Dipper
						BULBUL
						Red-whiskered Bulbul
						KINGLETS
						Golden-crowned Kinglet
						Ruby-crowned Kinglet
						WARBLERS
						Willow Warbler ▲
						Common Chiffchaff ▲
						Wood Warbler ▲
						Dusky Warbler ▲
						Pallas's Leaf Warbler ▲
						Yellow-browed Warbler ▲
						Arctic Warbler
						Kamchatka Leaf Warbler ▲
						Sedge Warbler ▲
						Blyth's Reed-Warbler ▲
						Middendorff's Grasshopper-Warbler ▲
						Lanceolated Warbler ▲
						Lesser Whitethroat ▲
						WRENTIT
						Wrentit
						FLYCATCHERS
						Spotted Flycatcher ▲
						Dark-sided Flycatcher ▲
						Asian Brown Flycatcher ▲
						Gray-streaked Flycatcher ▲
						Rufous-tailed Robin ▲

▲ RARE ■ EXTINCT

CHECKLIST

						Siberian Blue Robin ▲
						Bluethroat
						Siberian Rubythroat ▲
						Red-flanked Bluetail ▲
						Narcissus Flycatcher ▲
						Mugimaki Flycatcher ▲
						Taiga Flycatcher ▲
						Common Redstart ▲
						Stonechat ▲
						Northern Wheatear
						THRUSHES
						Eastern Bluebird
						Western Bluebird
						Mountain Bluebird
						Townsend's Solitaire
						Brown-backed Solitaire ▲
						Orange-billed Nightingale-Thrush ▲
						Black-headed Nightingale-Thrush ▲
						Veery
						Gray-cheeked Thrush
						Bicknell's Thrush
						Swainson's Thrush
						Hermit Thrush
						Wood Thrush
						Eurasian Blackbird ▲
						Eyebrowed Thrush ▲
						Dusky Thrush ▲
						Fieldfare ▲
						Redwing ▲
						Song Thrush ▲
						Clay-colored Thrush
						White-throated Thrush ▲

▲ RARE ■ EXTINCT

						Rufous-backed Robin
						American Robin
						Red-legged Thrush ▲
						Varied Thrush
						Aztec Thrush ▲
MOCKINGBIRDS AND THRASHERS						
						Blue Mockingbird ▲
						Gray Catbird
						Curve-billed Thrasher
						Brown Thrasher
						Long-billed Thrasher
						Bendire's Thrasher
						California Thrasher
						Le Conte's Thrasher
						Crissal Thrasher
						Sage Thrasher
						Bahama Mockingbird ▲
						Northern Mockingbird
STARLING AND MYNAH						
						European Starling
						Common Myna
ACCENTOR						
						Siberian Accentor ▲
WAGTAILS AND PIPITS						
						Eastern Yellow Wagtail
						Citrine Wagtail ▲
						Gray Wagtail ▲
						White Wagtail
						Tree Pipit ▲
						Olive-backed Pipit ▲
						Pechora Pipit ▲
						Red-throated Pipit ▲

▲ RARE ■ EXTINCT

						American Pipit
						Sprague's Pipit
WAXWINGS						
						Bohemian Waxwing
						Cedar Waxwing
SILKY FLYCATCHERS						
						Gray Silky-flycatcher ▲
						Phainopepla
OLIVE WARBLER						
						Olive Warbler
LONGSPURS						
						Lapland Longspur
						Chestnut-collared Longspur
						Smith's Longspur
						McCown's Longspur
						Snow Bunting
						McKay's Bunting
WOOD WARBLERS						
						Ovenbird
						Worm-eating Warbler
						Louisiana Waterthrush
						Northern Waterthrush
						Bachman's Warbler ■
						Golden-winged Warbler
						Blue-winged Warbler
						Black-and-white Warbler
						Prothonotary Warbler
						Swainson's Warbler
						Crescent-chested Warbler ▲
						Tennessee Warbler
						Orange-crowned Warbler
						Colima Warbler

▲ RARE ■ EXTINCT

						Lucy's Warbler
						Nashville Warbler
						Virginia's Warbler
						Connecticut Warbler
						Gray-crowned Yellowthroat ▲
						MacGillivray's Warbler
						Mourning Warbler
						Kentucky Warbler
						Common Yellowthroat
						Hooded Warbler
						American Redstart
						Kirtland's Warbler
						Cape May Warbler
						Cerulean Warbler
						Northern Parula
						Tropical Parula ▲
						Magnolia Warbler
						Bay-breasted Warbler
						Blackburnian Warbler
						Yellow Warbler
						Chestnut-sided Warbler
						Blackpoll Warbler
						Black-throated Blue Warbler
						Palm Warbler
						Pine Warbler
						Yellow-rumped Warbler
						Yellow-throated Warbler
						Prairie Warbler
						Grace's Warbler
						Black-throated Gray Warbler
						Townsend's Warbler
						Hermit Warbler

▲ RARE ■ EXTINCT

						Golden-cheeked Warbler
						Black-throated Green Warbler
						Fan-tailed Warbler ▲
						Rufous-capped Warbler ▲
						Golden-crowned Warbler ▲
						Canada Warbler
						Wilson's Warbler
						Red-faced Warbler
						Painted Redstart
						Slate-throated Redstart ▲
						Yellow-breasted Chat
						White-collared Seedeater ▲
BANANAQUIT						
						Bananaquit ▲
						Yellow-faced Grassquit ▲
						Black-faced Grassquit ▲
TRUE TANAGER						
						Western Spindalis ▲
EMBERIZINE SPARROWS						
						Rufous-winged Sparrow
						Botteri's Sparrow
						Cassin's Sparrow
						Bachman's Sparrow
						Grasshopper Sparrow
						Baird's Sparrow
						Henslow's Sparrow
						Le Conte's Sparrow
						Nelson's Sparrow
						Saltmarsh Sparrow
						Seaside Sparrow
						Olive Sparrow
						American Tree Sparrow

▲ RARE   ■ EXTINCT

						Chipping Sparrow
						Clay-colored Sparrow
						Black-chinned Sparrow
						Field Sparrow
						Brewer's Sparrow
						Worthen's Sparrow ▲
						Black-throated Sparrow
						Five-striped Sparrow
						Lark Sparrow
						Lark Bunting
						Fox Sparrow
						Dark-eyed Junco
						Yellow-eyed Junco
						White-crowned Sparrow
						Golden-crowned Sparrow
						Harris's Sparrow
						White-throated Sparrow
						Sagebrush Sparrow
						Bell's Sparrow
						Vesper Sparrow
						Savannah Sparrow
						Song Sparrow
						Lincoln's Sparrow
						Swamp Sparrow
						Canyon Towhee
						Abert's Towhee
						California Towhee
						Rufous-crowned Sparrow
						Green-tailed Towhee
						Spotted Towhee
						Eastern Towhee
						Pine Bunting ▲

▲ RARE ■ EXTINCT

							Yellow-browed Bunting ▲
							Little Bunting ▲
							Rustic Bunting ▲
							Yellow-throated Bunting ▲
							Yellow-breasted Bunting ▲
							Gray Bunting ▲
							Pallas's Bunting ▲
							Reed Bunting ▲
						CARDINALS	
						Hepatic Tanager	
						Summer Tanager	
						Scarlet Tanager	
						Western Tanager	
						Flame-colored Tanager ▲	
						Crimson-collared Grosbeak ▲	
						Northern Cardinal	
						Pyrrhuloxia	
						Yellow Grosbeak ▲	
						Rose-breasted Grosbeak	
						Black-headed Grosbeak	
						Blue Bunting ▲	
						Blue Grosbeak	
						Lazuli Bunting	
						Indigo Bunting	
						Varied Bunting	
						Painted Bunting	
						Dickcissel	
						ORIOLES AND BLACKBIRDS	
						Bobolink	
						Red-winged Blackbird	
						Tricolored Blackbird	
						Tawny-shouldered Blackbird ▲	

▲ RARE   ■ EXTINCT

CHECKLIST

						Western Meadowlark
						Eastern Meadowlark
						Yellow-headed Blackbird
						Rusty Blackbird
						Brewer's Blackbird
						Common Grackle
						Boat-tailed Grackle
						Great-tailed Grackle
						Shiny Cowbird ▲
						Bronzed Cowbird
						Brown-headed Cowbird
						Black-vented Oriole ▲
						Orchard Oriole
						Hooded Oriole
						Streak-backed Oriole ▲
						Bullock's Oriole
						Spot-breasted Oriole
						Altamira Oriole
						Audubon's Oriole
						Baltimore Oriole
						Scott's Oriole
						FINCHES
						Common Chaffinch ▲
						Brambling ▲
						Asian Rosy-Finch ▲
						Gray-crowned Rosy-Finch
						Black Rosy-Finch
						Brown-capped Rosy-Finch
						Pine Grosbeak
						Eurasian Bullfinch ▲
						House Finch
						Purple Finch

▲ RARE ■ EXTINCT

							Cassin's Finch
							Common Rosefinch ▲
							Pallas's Rosefinch ▲
							Oriental Greenfinch ▲
							Red Crossbill
							White-winged Crossbill
							Common Redpoll
							Hoary Redpoll
							Eurasian Siskin ▲
							Pine Siskin
							Lesser Goldfinch
							Lawrence's Goldfinch
							American Goldfinch
							Evening Grosbeak
							Hawfinch ▲
							OLD WORLD SPARROWS
							House Sparrow
							Eurasian Tree Sparrow
							MUNIA
							Scaly-breasted Munia

CHECKLIST

						NON-ESTABLISHED EXOTICS
						Swan Goose
						Bar-headed Goose
						Black Swan
						Ruddy Shelduck
						Common Shelduck
						Ringed Teal
						Mandarin Duck
						Red-crested Pochard
						Rosy-billed Pochard
						Helmeted Guineafowl
						Indian Peafowl
						Red Junglefowl
						Golden Pheasant
						Chilean Flamingo
						Greater Flamingo
						Lesser Flamingo
						Herald Petrel
						African Collared-Dove
						Sulphur-crested Cockatoo
						Cockatiel
						Rose-ringed Parakeet
						Budgerigar
						Yellow-chevroned Parakeet
						Lilac-crowned Parrot
						Red-lored Parrot
						Yellow-naped Parrot
						Yellow-headed Parrot
						Yellow-crowned Parrot
						Blue-fronted Parrot
						White-fronted Parrot
						Mealy Parrot

▲ RARE ■ EXTINCT

CHECKLIST

						Orange-winged Parrot
						Dusky-headed Parakeet
						Blue-and-yellow Macaw
						Chestnut-fronted Macaw
						Blue-crowned Parakeet
						Mitred Parakeet
						Red-masked Parakeet
						White-eyed Parakeet
						Green Parakeet
						Black-throated Magpie-Jay
						House Crow
						Hooded Crow
						Eurasian Blue Tit
						Great Tit
						Red-vented Bulbul
						Japanese White-eye
						Hill Myna
						Crested Myna
						Red-crested Cardinal
						European Goldfinch
						Yellow-fronted Canary
						Orange Bishop
						Orange-cheeked Waxbill
						Bronze Mannikin
						Tricolored Munia
						Java Sparrow
						Pin-tailed Whydah

▲ RARE ■ EXTINCT

CHECKLIST

▲ RARE ■ EXTINCT

CHECKLIST

LIFE LIST

1	
2	
3	
4	
5	
6	
7	
8	
9	
10	
11	
12	
13	
14	
15	
16	
17	
18	
19	
20	
21	
22	
23	
24	
25	
26	
27	
28	
29	
30	
31	
32	

LIFE LIST

33	
34	
35	
36	
37	
38	
39	
40	
41	
42	
43	
44	
45	
46	
47	
48	
49	
50	
51	
52	
53	
54	
55	
56	
57	
58	
59	
60	
61	
62	
63	
64	

LIFE LIST

65	
66	
67	
68	
69	
70	
71	
72	
73	
74	
75	
76	
77	
78	
79	
80	
81	
82	
83	
84	
85	
86	
87	
88	
89	
90	
91	
92	
93	
94	
95	
96	

97	
98	
99	
100	
101	
102	
103	
104	
105	
106	
107	
108	
109	
110	
111	
112	
113	
114	
115	
116	
117	
118	
119	
120	
121	
122	
123	
124	
125	
126	
127	
128	

129	
130	
131	
132	
133	
134	
135	
136	
137	
138	
139	
140	
141	
142	
143	
144	
145	
146	
147	
148	
149	
150	
151	
152	
153	
154	
155	
156	
157	
158	
159	
160	

LIFE LIST

161
162
163
164
165
166
167
168
169
170
171
172
173
174
175
176
177
178
179
180
181
182
183
184
185
186
187
188
189
190
191
192

193	
194	
195	
196	
197	
198	
199	
200	
201	
202	
203	
204	
205	
206	
207	
208	
209	
210	
211	
212	
213	
214	
215	
216	
217	
218	
219	
220	
221	
222	
223	
224	

LIFE LIST

225
226
227
228
229
230
231
232
233
234
235
236
237
238
239
240
241
242
243
244
245
246
247
248
249
250
251
252
253
254
255
256

257	
258	
259	
260	
261	
262	
263	
264	
265	
266	
267	
268	
269	
270	
271	
272	
273	
274	
275	
276	
277	
278	
279	
280	
281	
282	
283	
284	
285	
286	
287	
288	

289	
290	
291	
292	
293	
294	
295	
296	
297	
298	
299	
300	
301	
302	
303	
304	
305	
306	
307	
308	
309	
310	
311	
312	
313	
314	
315	
316	
317	
318	
319	
320	

321	
322	
323	
324	
325	
326	
327	
328	
329	
330	
331	
332	
333	
334	
335	
336	
337	
338	
339	
340	
341	
342	
343	
344	
345	
346	
347	
348	
349	
350	
351	
352	

353	
354	
355	
356	
357	
358	
359	
360	
361	
362	
363	
364	
365	
366	
367	
368	
369	
370	
371	
372	
373	
374	
375	
376	
377	
378	
379	
380	
381	
382	
383	
384	

385	
386	
387	
388	
389	
390	
391	
392	
393	
394	
395	
396	
397	
398	
399	
400	
401	
402	
403	
404	
405	
406	
407	
408	
409	
410	
411	
412	
413	
414	
415	
416	

417	
418	
419	
420	
421	
422	
423	
424	
425	
426	
427	
428	
429	
430	
431	
432	
433	
434	
435	
436	
437	
438	
439	
440	
441	
442	
443	
444	
445	
446	
447	
448	

449	
450	
451	
452	
453	
454	
455	
456	
457	
458	
459	
460	
461	
462	
463	
464	
465	
466	
467	
468	
469	
470	
471	
472	
473	
474	
475	
476	
477	
478	
479	
480	

481	
482	
483	
484	
485	
486	
487	
488	
489	
490	
491	
492	
493	
494	
495	
496	
497	
498	
499	
500	
501	
502	
503	
504	
505	
506	
507	
508	
509	
510	
511	
512	

513	
514	
515	
516	
517	
518	
519	
520	
521	
522	
523	
524	
525	
526	
527	
528	
529	
530	
531	
532	
533	
534	
535	
536	
537	
538	
539	
540	
541	
542	
543	
544	

545	
546	
547	
548	
549	
550	
551	
552	
553	
554	
555	
556	
557	
558	
559	
560	
561	
562	
563	
564	
565	
566	
567	
568	
569	
570	
571	
572	
573	
574	
575	
576	

LIFE LIST

577	
578	
579	
580	
581	
582	
583	
584	
585	
586	
587	
588	
589	
590	
591	
592	
593	
594	
595	
596	
597	
598	
599	
600	
601	
602	
603	
604	
605	
606	
607	
608	

609	
610	
611	
612	
613	
614	
615	
616	
617	
618	
619	
620	
621	
622	
623	
624	
625	
626	
627	
628	
629	
630	
631	
632	
633	
634	
635	
636	
637	
638	
639	
640	

641	
642	
643	
644	
645	
646	
647	
648	
649	
650	
651	
652	
653	
654	
655	
656	
657	
658	
659	
660	
661	
662	
663	
664	
665	
666	
667	
668	
669	
670	
671	
672	

673	
674	
675	
676	
677	
678	
679	
680	
681	
682	
683	
684	
685	
686	
687	
688	
689	
690	
691	
692	
693	
694	
695	
696	
697	
698	
699	
700	
701	
702	
703	
704	

LIFE LIST

705	
706	
707	
708	
709	
710	
711	
712	
713	
714	
715	
716	
717	
718	
719	
720	
721	
722	
723	
724	
725	
726	
727	
728	
729	
730	
731	
732	
733	
734	
735	
736	

737	
738	
739	
740	
741	
742	
743	
744	
745	
746	
747	
748	
749	
750	
751	
752	
753	
754	
755	
756	
757	
758	
759	
760	
761	
762	
763	
764	
765	
766	
767	
768	

769	
770	
771	
772	
773	
774	
775	
776	
777	
778	
779	
780	
781	
782	
783	
784	
785	
786	
787	
788	
789	
790	
791	
792	
793	
794	
795	
796	
797	
798	
799	
800	

LIFE LIST

801	
802	
803	
804	
805	
806	
807	
808	
809	
810	
811	
812	
813	
814	
815	
816	
817	
818	
819	
820	
821	
822	
823	
824	
825	
826	
827	
828	
829	
830	
831	
832	

833	
834	
835	
836	
837	
838	
839	
840	
841	
842	
843	
844	
845	
846	
847	
848	
849	
850	
851	
852	
853	
854	
855	
856	
857	
858	
859	
860	
861	
862	
863	
864	

865
866
867
868
869
870
871
872
873
874
875
876
877
878
879
880
881
882
883
884
885
886
887
888
889
890
891
892
893
894
895
896

897	
898	
899	
900	
901	
902	
903	
904	
905	
906	
907	
908	
909	
910	
911	
912	
913	
914	
915	
916	
917	
918	
919	
920	
921	
922	
923	
924	
925	
926	
927	
928	

LIFE LIST

929	
930	
931	
932	
933	
934	
935	
936	
937	
938	
939	
940	
941	
942	
943	
944	
945	
946	
947	
948	
949	
950	
951	
952	
953	
954	
955	
956	
957	
958	
959	
960	

LIFE LIST

961	
962	
963	
964	
965	
966	
967	
968	
969	
970	
971	
972	
973	
974	
975	
976	
977	
978	
979	
980	
981	
982	
983	
984	
985	
986	
987	
988	
989	
990	
991	
992	

LIFE LIST

993	
994	
995	
996	
997	
998	
999	
1000	
1001	
1002	
1003	
1004	
1005	
1006	
1007	
1008	
1009	
1010	
1011	
1012	
1013	
1014	
1015	
1016	
1017	
1018	
1019	
1020	
1021	
1022	
1023	
1024	

ABA Code of Ethics

1. Promote the welfare of birds and their environment.

1(a) Support the protection of important bird habitat.

1(b) To avoid stressing birds or exposing them to danger, exercise restraint and caution during observation, photography, sound recording, or filming.

Limit the use of recordings and other methods of attracting birds, and never use such methods in heavily birded areas or for attracting any species that is Threatened, Endangered, or of Special Concern, or is rare in your local area.

Keep well back from nests and nesting colonies, roosts, display areas, and important feeding sites. In such sensitive areas, if there is a need for extended observation, photography, filming, or recording, try to use a blind or hide, and take advantage of natural cover.

Use artificial light sparingly for filming or photography, especially for close-ups.

1(c) Before advertising the presence of a rare bird, evaluate the potential for disturbance to the bird, its surroundings, and other people in the area, and proceed only if access can be controlled, disturbance can be minimized, and permission has been obtained from private land-owners. The sites of rare nesting birds should be divulged only to the proper conservation authorities.

1(d) Stay on roads, trails, and paths where they exist; otherwise keep habitat disturbance to a minimum.

2. Respect the law and the rights of others.

2(a) Do not enter private property without the owner's explicit permission.

2(b) Follow all laws, rules, and regulations governing use of roads and public areas, both at home and abroad.

2(c) Practice common courtesy in contacts with other people. Your exemplary behavior will generate goodwill with birders and non-birders alike.

3. Ensure that feeders, nest structures, and other artificial bird environments are safe.

3(a) Keep dispensers, water, and food clean and free of decay or disease. It is important to feed birds continually during harsh weather.

3(b) Maintain and clean nest structures regularly.

3(c) If you are attracting birds to an area, ensure the birds are not exposed to predation from cats and other domestic animals, or dangers posed by artificial hazards.

4. Group birding, whether organized or impromptu, requires special care.

Each individual in the group, in addition to the obligations spelled out in Items #1 and #2, has responsibilities as a Group Member.

4(a) Respect the interests, rights, and skills of fellow birders as well as those of people participating in other legitimate outdoor activities. Freely share your knowledge and experience, except where code 1(c) applies. Be especially helpful to beginning birders.

4(b) If you witness unethical birding behavior, assess the situation and intervene if you think it prudent. When interceding, inform the person(s) of the inappropriate action and attempt, within reason, to have it stopped. If the behavior continues, document it and notify appropriate individuals or organizations.

Group Leader Responsibilities [amateur and professional trips and tours]

4(c) Be an exemplary ethical role model for the group. Teach through word and example.

4(d) Keep groups to a size that limits impact on the environment and does not interfere with others using the same area.

4(e) Ensure everyone in the group knows of and practices this code.

4(f) Learn and inform the group of any special circumstances applicable to the areas being visited (e.g. no sound devices allowed).

4(g) Acknowledge that professional tour companies bear a special responsibility to place the welfare of birds and the benefits of public knowledge ahead of the companys' commercial interests. Ideally, leaders should keep track of tour sightings, document unusual occurrences, and submit records to appropriate organizations.

Index